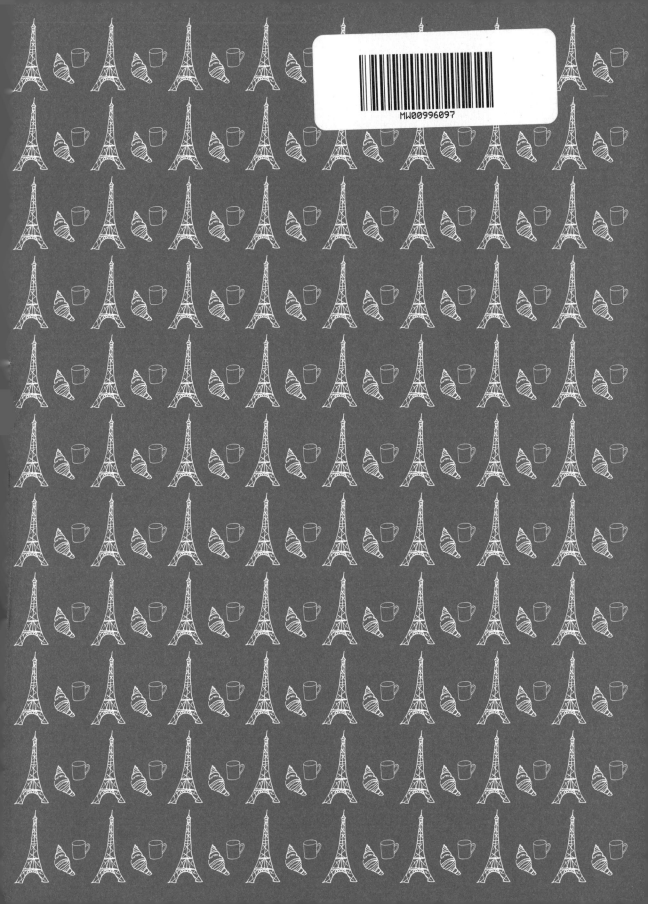

Creative
Paris

MY
LITTLE
PARIS

Creative
Paris

URBAN INTERIORS • INSPIRING INNOVATORS

by

Clémence Barbier
Anne-Flore Chapellier
Marie Doyen-Monpoix
Maxime Froissant
Clémentine Godais
Camille Gross
Anne-Sophie Leroux
Tomoko Yasuda

Flammarion

Contents

INTRODUCING *My Little Paris*

Back in 2008, when the first email revealing a secret address in Paris was sent to a close circle of friends, no one suspected it would grow into My Little Paris— an online sensation that today reaches more than four million subscribers, with media and e-commerce activities. Covering the most exciting underground and up-and-coming trends, tips, and addresses in the City of Light, My Little Paris has its finger on the pulse like no other, providing bright ideas and fresh lifestyle inspiration to a cool and clued-in audience.

Today, the My Little Paris team welcomes us inside their creative universe, offering a novel and intimate glimpse behind the scenes where their creativity flourishes. They open the doors to their homes and workspaces, reveal where they find their innovative energy, and invite us to share their favorite places around town.

Welcome to the *real* Paris!

THE SPIRIT *of place*

___

We all have our favorite places—special spots that nourish the soul.
These places, in turn, leave their mark on us in subtle but lasting ways.

The space that surrounds us has a direct impact on our behavior, our attitude, and our energy. We know that forest bathing soothes the spirit. Contemplating natural, wide-open spaces—a mountain landscape, the sun setting over the ocean—lets the brain "rest." Similarly, the layout of the spaces where we work every day or come home to each night can stifle our creativity—or, conversely, enhance it.

The spirit of Paris has a powerful effect on both visitors and those who live here. The Haussmann-style buildings are home to apartments where Parisians take time to entertain, to decorate, to love. Paris is one of those rare capital cities where the inhabitants open their homes for dinner or cocktails with friends. Regardless of how many square feet they occupy, these places attest to the creativity that Parisians bring to their way of life. For a peek into their "home sweet home," at their hardwood floors, molded ceilings, and fireplaces, for a glimpse of their private chaos, we chose the Parisians we know best: the teams, friends, and family who form the heart of My Little Paris.

It's not just our homes that affect our mood. That's why we wanted to create a work space at My Little Paris that reflects our personality. We set up shop in a place that manufactured dreams for many years: a former merry-go-round factory. And we furnished it with ideas instead of desks and chairs, so that these ideas would generate other ideas, other projects, and other desires. Creativity loves nothing better than abundance.

This book invites you to visit former servants' quarters tucked under the rooftops, apartments that sit cozily nestled next to the Sacré-Coeur, offices in Paris, Berlin, and Tokyo, and more—the creative spaces where we've invested so much of ourselves. Things aren't always tidy, but we're thrilled to have you come in for a visit.

— The My Little Paris team

AT HOME

LOLA
Editor in Chief

—

NATION

Having studied in Sweden and landed her first job at the advertising agency BETC, Lola now oversees Tapage. Aimed at millennials, this app, which highlights the coolest bars, restaurants, and stores in the French capital, had already reached a million downloads. She also added a newsletter and Instagram and Facebook accounts to the brand, all with one lofty ambition in mind: to give a voice to those women who don't have one yet/really/at all. They include inspired artists and social activists, but also (of course) her readers.

Her small sixth-floor apartment looks like a fashion designer's showroom. A busy one. Who said clothes belong in the closet? At Lola's place, they're vacuum-packed in the kitchen and rolled up in the bathroom. Her fashion bible—her first brush with style—is *Fresh Fruits*. She stumbled into fashion at the age of eleven, and has stayed there ever since. She's worked as a model for Vivienne Westwood and a saleswoman at Margiela, and is now adored by Jacquemus. She starts each day with a selfie in the elevator. It's her "fashion breakfast," as she calls it.

"I used to live in the Marais. I'd have to wait forever just to get a baguette. Here, it's hi-thanks-bye. It's not quite gentrified yet; it feels a little like Shoreditch did fifteen years ago. When I got here, I threw a lot of parties, all the time. Avoiding the neighbor was a commando mission. One day she cornered me in the elevator; I didn't know what to do with myself. She said, 'Is your father's name Nicolas? And is your mother Marie-Noëlle?' It turns out she was a childhood friend of my parents; they'd had a wild time together when they were eighteen. My place is small. But with the view, you can imagine that you're in the great outdoors. That's great. There are no buildings opposite my windows. I can walk around naked."

"My first designer piece was a pair of Margiela ankle boots, the Tabi Boots. I saved up for a year to buy them! I have a big, light-filled kitchen. It's stupid because I don't cook. I keep my ankle boots in there."

"This is a ring Martin Margiela gave me for my twenty-second birthday. I don't wear it anymore, it's become a talisman. It's always on my mantel. I don't feel at home if it's not in its place."

"I'm obsessed with cats. This is a Maneki Neko. In Japanese culture, it's a good-luck charm. I sort of feel like it keeps watch over me. Actually, it's not from Japan. I bought it in Madrid."

"I love candy. This is my dream dinner. But I'm an adult, so I have to eat vegetables."

"I have at least a hundred pairs of earrings. You'll never see me without a pair."

CLÉMENTINE

Creative Director

———

NOUVELLE ATHÈNES

Clémentine first learned her trade at Central Saint Martins in London, where she arrived with a love for beautiful clothes—especially clothes that are liberating. She wasn't an obvious fit for her role at My Little Paris, and a few feathers were ruffled, but the happy result was that colleagues were inspired to even greater feats of creativity. Her go-to books? *Gamestorming* by Dave Gray, Sunni Brown, and James Macanufo, *A Brief History of Time* by Stephen Hawking, and *The Power of Now* by Eckhart Tolle. Oh, and we nearly forgot: the pull-out pages of the French children's magazine *Astrapi*.

In her apartment, flashy cushions sit like pom-poms on a washed-linen coverlet, and Japanese masks buddy up to a contemporary painting. All these little objects jostle for space. Never take anything seriously, is her advice. You can run on organic kombucha *and* splurge at McDonald's. Her motto? "An apple a day keeps the doctor away, as long as you have good aim." That says it all: anything goes.

"As far as interior design is concerned, I have no rules. Spaces, objects, even types of food can bring you joy. I like the handmade, the man-made, the made-in-France-with-love, the made-in-China, the vintage, the swapped, the found-in-the-street.... As long as it makes you happy, it's worth keeping. That's what counts at the end of the day."

"Cushions are where it's at! I have a lot of cushions. Everywhere. They move around. They follow you wherever you go. Piled up, they're like a pillowy cloud for dreaming on. Or working on, or meditating on. Oh yes, there are cushions for every occasion. I'm telling you, cushions are everything!"

"I see my apartment as a birdcage, open and bright. There's always something going on, all day long; people peck at food, pass through, leave and come back. It's noisy, and sometimes feathers fly. But in the evening, when the kids are in bed, everything becomes peaceful again. I like the idea that your house is like a market filled with a thousand little treasures, some of them unexpected."

"I'm sensitive to small details, to the great efforts that people go to in their daily lives. I have a secret list of ordinary people I find inspiring. For example, there's Marcel. He's a sort of shy Hercules with a mustache, who manages a grocery store on the regional D955 road from 6 a.m. to 8 p.m., seven days a week, and delivers to customers with reduced mobility. He's a big-hearted hero."

"I choose my kimonos for their patterns and colors. Their length requires a slow, precise step. The sleeves make for ample, graceful movements. The overall shape is soft and elegant."

"Hats equal adventure. My idol, Indiana Jones, wears one. I like Borsalino hats in winter, but I prefer multicolored paper hats the rest of the year. Yes, paper hats, like the ones kids make!"

"Mobiles, kites—I love anything that flies. Earrings too! They're like architecture in miniature. They're worn close to the eyes and mouth, but you can't see them. Nonetheless, they somehow bring everything together."

"This fish vase just joined my vase collection. It's blue inside. I love that someone had the idea of painting the inside of a vase sky blue! It's the kind of detail that makes you smile when you notice it for the first time. So no big bouquets for this vase—just a few flowers."

"Peggy Guggenheim was a complete person. It's thanks to her flaws that we get a glimpse of who she really was. People criticize her for being a 'nymphomaniac,' but if she'd been a man I'm sure everyone would have approved. There's something endearing about her, because she wasn't concerned about her image, she was just true to herself. I find her extremely contemporary and inspiring: a liberated, opportunistic, courageous, generous woman who made her own luck."

JULIA
Events Project Manager

—

ABBESSES

She works miracles using just a few odds and ends, and her address book is the most envied in Paris. Julia stages the kind of unique, unforgettable event that leaves you gobsmacked. Consider her a fairy godmother to the present moment. She used to work at The Bristol hotel, where she met her partner, Thomas. He was a sommelier, and she managed the restaurants. Looking after others is in their blood. Their apartment is also generous and uncomplaining. It accommodates an open-air wine cellar on every shelf. It makes no comment when there's a wine stain on the hardwood flooring. It lets in light through the wisteria in the morning, when it's time for coffee. It even watches over Thomas as he sleeps; he works night shifts and gets home just as Julia is slipping out the door.

*"The living room is full of bottles . . .
empty ones. I'm not allowed to put
flowers in them. So we have a deal:
no more than twenty-five bottles at any
one time. One for every 10 square feet
(1m²) is already quite a lot!"*

"When Thomas moved in, I gave him a rather unique gift: my cellar! It used to be my junk room, I shoved all kinds of things in there. Now it's a wine cellar, very organized. My dad even installed a reinforced door."

"The last good bottle
we opened was a 2014
Noël de Montbenault
by Richard Leroy, to
celebrate the opening
of Thomas's restaurant,
Vantre. He's an associate
sommelier. Beyoncé
swears by their gnocchi
when she's in town."

"This is my 'Polaroid'
mirror, surrounded by
old and recent photos.
My sister and I
messed around
restaging the same
pictures we'd taken
twenty years ago.
The old Polaroids
hold up better, actually.
Just like good wine."

"I love Agatha Christie mysteries.
They help me relax. I'm crazy about
them. I even have several editions
of the same book."

MAXIME
Editor in Chief

—

LA MOUZAÏA

What does being editor in chief involve, exactly? Above all, you have to be able to communicate your enthusiasm, convincing as many people as possible to discover for themselves something you really love. This is what Maxime does for the 250,000 readers of the website Merci Alfred. But he also saves some of his energy for hiking in the mountains during his vacations and singing opera the rest of the year.

Looking to safeguard his downtime, Maxime went for a radical solution. His choice of neighborhood, La Mouzaïa (otherwise known as "a bit of countryside in Paris"), is connected to the rest of the city by the 7 bis metro line, the quietest in the capital. It's both in Paris and at the same time feels miles away. Of course, this impression is reinforced if, like Maxime, you choose not to have Internet. So much for YouTube, and all the better for curling up with a good book.

"The best thing about this apartment is that it's not connected to the Internet. That leaves so much time for everything else: listening to music, reading, letting your mind wander. I like displaying books face out: their front covers are like an invitation to dive inside."

"My apartment is a starting point for mental wanderings, but also for real outings: in the evenings, map in hand, I compare advice from different guidebooks and prepare my hiking trips. Some happen, others never materialize. It's not the destination but the journey—sometimes even just the planning—that matters. I work on newsletters for Merci Alfred in the same way, treating them as starting points rather than destinations."

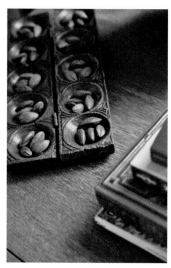

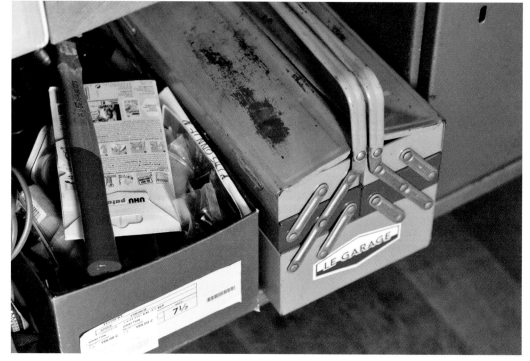

"For me, the journey begins the moment you pack your bag. My hiking backpack is super-optimized: I know exactly what to put in it and in what order. I can do it almost without thinking about it."

"I've always liked poetry very much; then, one day, I discovered Schubert's lieder: poetry put to music. It's a little like going from reading plays to seeing them performed."

"For many people, the Tour de France is just a bunch of guys pedaling on bikes. To me it means more than that: it's a saga to follow year after year, scrutinizing preparations ahead of time. It's (almost) better than Game of Thrones."

"Whether you're putting together a hike or building a shelf, it comes down to the same thing. You have to plan ahead. That's probably why my maps and my toolbox are next to each other."

"My favorite book, The Atlas of Remote Islands, tells the story of islands that were depopulated following catastrophes. It's incredibly nostalgic in feel, and the book itself is beautiful."

LILI

Journalist and Author

BLANCHE

A former beauty editor at *Vogue* magazine, Lili worked at *M*, the magazine of *Le Monde* newspaper, for four years, writing topical articles about fragrances and cosmetics. Seven years ago, she launched a lifestyle blog and became an expert in "me time," advising readers on how to transform daily rituals into precious moments. In her book *Pimp My Breakfast*, preparing the morning meal becomes an art form. It comes as no surprise that, for her, interior design is almost like a religion.

It took her months to decide on the colors for her apartment. To make matters more difficult, Lili doesn't let herself be influenced by trends. Those Moroccan rugs you see in every Parisian living room? Very nice in Essaouira, but that's where they should stay. Her essential reference is Junichirō Tanizaki's *In Praise of Shadows*, an essay on Japanese aesthetics and its treatment of light. Try picking out a lamp after reading that.

"I turned breakfast into a kind of ritual. Obviously my
kitchen isn't this beautiful every morning: I don't
always have the time or the inclination to arrange fruit
in my acai bowl. But when I do it, strangely enough,
I have a different kind of day. Time for myself is never
wasted time."

"Our couch is an invitation to sprawl. I dream of having a couch by India Mahdavi, but I can't let this one go. When my daughter Jeanne was a baby, she fit perfectly in the folds, which doesn't make chucking it out on the sidewalk any easier."

"The colors on the walls change all the time, sometimes after just a year. The 'Pink Ground' in my bathroom is the only one I've never gotten bored of. It's my favorite room; I meditate there every morning at dawn."

"This is the Barbie from the Hitchcock film **The Birds**. I bought it at Colette's a long time ago; I love it. Her pale green suit, her vintage handbag.... She's unbelievable."

"There are candles everywhere in my apartment. This one (above) is important: every day it reminds me to mind my words and my dreams. We should try to write down everything that makes us feel alive. I try to keep a journal of my emotions."

"I'm very fond of ceramics by Astier de Villatte and collect their pieces. My tea addiction more than justifies the number of teapots I have in the kitchen."

"These drawings are by my husband, Bastien. He's an artist. He painted this image of a young girl well before our daughter Jeanne was born. But it looks very much like her. It's unsettling. It's as if she was already in his mind."

ANA
Director of e-Commerce

—

DAUMESNIL

Ana, who looks after the My Little Box subscription service around the world, gets up early in Paris, lunches in Berlin, and goes to sleep in Tokyo. Since her days unfold over several time zones, she keeps her feet firmly on the ground by referring to *The Power of Moments* by Chip and Dan Heath. The authors explain how a single experience can change a life—the same philosophy she uses to surprise 150,000 box subscribers each and every month.

Ana does everything differently: she doesn't live in a typical Haussmann-style neighborhood, and her living room doesn't have a hardwood floor—it's covered in sea rush, just like a vacation home. And yet Ana is one of a rare breed, a true Parisian who grew up in the city and has always lived in the twelfth arrondissement. Her apartment is full of vintage objects, like many others, only here they're actual family heirlooms. A lithograph by a great-aunt, a famous Argentinian artist, jostles for space with leather-bound volumes from the family's collection and a watercolor by an architect friend. Ana doesn't tell stories—she collects objects and lets them do the talking instead. That's her talent, and she's made a career out of it.

"From my trips to Japan I brought back a taste for very clean, minimalist design. I travel there regularly to meet with our team. Working with Japan is a daily challenge, but now that we've succeeded we can go anywhere!"

"I'm an early riser. I manage to get a lot done in the mornings. I watch a TED conference every day, then I knit, I embroider. I'm currently making a tablecloth. I feel relaxed when I don't have to think about anything; it's like a private meditation session."

"I'm really looking forward to having a big table so I can have friends over for dinner. At the moment it's pretty much just finger food, but once I have the table it'll be starter-main-dessert mode. In Paris, you become a real adult once you have a dining room."

MY LITTLE BOX

"I've always got a book by Marguerite Duras on the go, alongside something else. I know them by heart. These are my first Pléiades volumes. The others are in my parents' collection. We share."

"I got this bottle with its label designed by Kanako when I signed my contract with My Little Paris."

"I travel to Spain once a year to visit family in Zamora, in Castile. So I stock up with delicacies for the year."

"This year's birthday present: shipping-container boxes from the My Little Box team. I love them! I love ports; they're constantly alive with enormous machines that 99 percent of people are completely unaware of. I try to visit one a year."

"I have a passion for Repetto: I got my first pair when I turned seventeen. They were flats. I'm still a loyal follower, but I've moved up to the kitten-heel version."

MARIE-YAÉ

Illustrator and Ceramicist

BEHIND STATION F
START-UP CAMPUS

Marie-Yaé sure gets out there. Her departure gate was Les Arts Décoratifs in Paris, where she studied for several years. Her illustrations then took her to Kyoto, on the other side of the world, where one day she just happened to take a pottery class. She continued with ceramics once she was back in Paris, turning the studio next door into her second home, where she juggles paper, pencils, gouache, clay, vases, bowls, and more. Her favorite book is *The Baron in the Trees*—even if she hasn't actually read it. (A friend told her the story, chapter by chapter, during a long trip on the Trans-Siberian Railway.) At home, her windows open onto a big garden, which helps provide fresh inspiration. In the spring, the cherry tree floods her studio with petals and reminds her of Kyoto. From her time in that city, she also has Nicolas Bouvier's *The Japanese Chronicles*, her second favorite book. It features this sentence, which she has taken as her motto: "You think you're going to make a trip, but soon the trip is making you—or unmaking you."

"If I ran into a genie who asked me to choose any museum in the world, I would pick the Barnes Foundation in Philadelphia. Barnes was a pharmacist who had an incredible collection of paintings: sixty works by Cézanne, twenty or so by Henri Rousseau, Picasso, Matisse, and others. He was a real enthusiast."

*"Hands down, the two people who inspire me
the most are Sonia Kronlund and Ira Glass,
producers of the radio shows* Les Pieds sur
Terre *(France Culture) and* This American
Life *(National Public Radio), respectively.
I listen to podcasts all the time when I'm working,
to get other people's perspectives."*

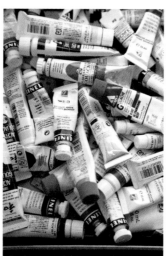

"I picture my ideal studio as being in a garden, a very large garden full of trees. I can also see myself in the Atelier Brancusi at the Centre Pompidou. At the moment I'm looking for another studio so that I can be surrounded by new people. I need new things around me. I also have an unusual fantasy: I dream of making charms—little charms that go in the galette cakes we eat at Epiphany! In a new environment I'd feel freer to start new projects."

"I stole this glass from the bar where we celebrated our graduation. I couldn't just leave, I had to take a souvenir with me. My Japanese aunt gave me this cup, which she made herself. It has the biggest handle in the world, it looks like an elephant; it's so practical."

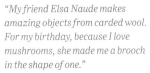

"My friend Elsa Naude makes amazing objects from carded wool. For my birthday, because I love mushrooms, she made me a brooch in the shape of one."

◀ "In one of my favorite supply stores in Kyoto, one of the sales staff had made this little sleeping figure to show what you can do with modeling clay. I loved it so much, he gave it to me at the end of my trip. Now it watches over my lemon tree."

"It's odd … but I keep this bag with me everywhere I go. My grandmother in Japan made it out of old kimonos."

AMANDINE

Cofounder of My Little Paris

BUTTE BERGEYRE

As a writer for My Little Paris, it is Amandine's job to find the right words to inspire four million readers every single day. She's also responsible for hunting down the city's hottest spots. There was, for instance, that 1950s restaurant, forgotten at the end of a sleepy cul-de-sac. She went there on a whim—and discovered that the owner planned to close down only two days later. After Amandine's newsletter had gone out, however, he was booked solid for a month. Amandine rejects routine as boring and helps energize Parisians as they go about their daily lives. And when she needs inspiration herself, she dives into Nicolas Delesalle's book *Un Parfum d'herbe coupée* (The Scent of Cut Grass). She's read it forty-five times and isn't done yet.

Visiting the top floor of Amandine's home is like standing on the bridge of ship, with Sacré-Coeur on the horizon. Her neighborhood, the Butte Bergeyre, is unique. The baker visits once a week and honks his horn, supplying croissants and baguettes to residents. When the weather is nice, the rooftop terraces come to life, deck chairs are unfolded, and residents sit down to casual dinners that stretch out into long, lazy evenings. Below, the front doors are locked, and the neighborhood communicates from rooftop to rooftop.

"You could write a book about the Butte Bergeyre. Originally, it was a fairground. Then it became a sports stadium, whose star rugby player was Robert Bergeyre. He died on the front line in 1914. In the 1930s, they tore down the stadium and built housing with flat roofs for workers. The neighborhood was inaugurated by Joséphine Baker."

"I arrived here on my own four years ago, and now there are four of us. The house makes me happy. When I visited it for the first time, the real-estate agent said, 'It's a real rabbit warren,' referring to its five small floors. I was smitten."

"This place makes you want to write. In fact, every time I start a text for My Little Paris, I like to imagine it's the first sentence of a book. Those opening lines have to be crafted very carefully."

"My favorite passage from my favorite book, Un Parfum d'herbe coupée *(The Scent of Cut Grass)."*

"These dishes belonged to my paternal grandmother. They're called "talking plates." Originally, they were intended to encourage conversation at the dinner table and make the guests feel relaxed."

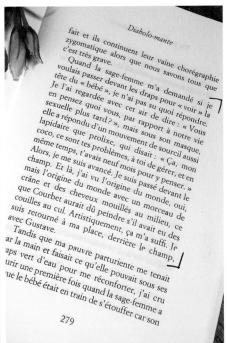

Diabolo-mante

fait et ils continuent leur vaine chorégraphie zygomatique alors que nous savons tous que c'est très grave.

Quand la sage-femme m'a demandé si je voulais passer devant les draps pour « voir » la tête du « bébé », je n'ai pas su quoi répondre. Je l'ai regardée avec cet air de dire : « Vous en pensez quoi vous, par rapport à notre vie sexuelle plus tard ? », mais sous son masque, elle a répondu d'un mouvement de sourcil aussi lapidaire que prolixe, qui disait : « Ça, mon coco, ce sont tes problèmes, à toi de gérer, et en même temps, t'avais neuf mois pour y penser. » Alors, je me suis avancé. Je suis passé devant le champ. Et là, j'ai vu l'origine du monde, oui, mais l'origine du monde avec un morceau de crâne et des cheveux mouillés au milieu, ce que Courbet aurait dû peindre s'il avait eu des couilles au cul. Artistiquement, ça m'a suffi. Je suis retourné à ma place, derrière le champ, avec Gustave.

Tandis que ma pauvre parturiente me tenait par la main et faisait ce qu'elle pouvait sous les draps vert d'eau pour me réconforter, j'ai cru mourir une première fois quand la sage-femme a vue le bébé était en train de s'étouffer car son

279

"Those mustard glasses from the sixties.... They're from my childhood; my maternal grandmother kept them."

"This comic book reveals what it's like behind the scenes at the Michelin Guide *and tells the story of one of the first female food critics. It combines my two loves: Japan and eating."*

LE GOÛT D'EMMA

◀ *"A friend at My Little Paris gave this to me when I moved in here. It's the perfect housewarming gift: four phrases that sum up a person's tastes."*

"These are solar-powered lightbulbs. They have a light sensor and come on exactly when night falls, as though they were responsible for plunging Paris into darkness. When the windows and streets light up, I come up to the terrace to savor the moment."

CÉLINE

Greenery Designer

—

JULES JOFFRIN

Céline first started out in the music industry, working as a venue scheduler. Today, however, her job is to supply greenery to a roster of recipents, from private clients and offices to television studios and film sets. Every morning at 5 a.m., she parks her truck at Rungis wholesale market and, perched on her high heels, selects the most beautiful specimens. Then she crisscrosses Paris, calling in at large gardens and tiny balconies along the way. She never stops. Especially not when she gets home.

In her family compound in the eighteenth arrondissement, Céline specializes in adoptions. She adopts her children's friends for movie nights, takes in neighbors for impromptu barbecues, finds a home for objects in need of upscaling. Her home resembles Noah's Ark: in addition to her four children, there's a dog, a cat, a tortoise, and a snail. There are lots of people, but there's enough space for everyone. In the 1920s, her apartment was a factory that manufactured movie posters. Artists drew by hand on sheets of paper suspended from the high ceilings, where Céline's plants now thrive.

"When we arrived, the kids and I essentially camped
in the house for a year. We ate on a tablecloth on the
floor, we slept in the same room. We're settled in now,
but we've kept the improvised DIY feel. For example,
the older kids share a dormitory and I use a wooden
plank next to my bathtub to convert it into a desk."

"This is my most kitsch object (below). It's the same dachshund my great-aunt had on the rear deck of her 2CV. He has a nodding head! He kept me entertained in traffic jams as a child."

"I have two foolproof techniques for cooking: the first is my 'dump-everything-in' salad to use up the previous day's leftovers. The other is a wonderful cookbook by Caroline Pessin that explains how to prepare a week's worth of meals in two hours."

INÈS
Strategic Planner

CANAL SAINT-MARTIN

You could say that Inès lives in the future. Her job as a strategic planner is always to stay a few steps ahead. If she had the choice, every year she'd make the trip to Austin, Texas, to attend South by Southwest, the world's most innovative fair for new technology and interactive media.

She's always thinking of the city of tomorrow, even if her apartment on the banks of the Canal Saint-Martin anchors her firmly to the Paris of today. Inès goes to work on foot, a twenty-minute walk down the ugliest boulevard in the capital. She finds the journey stimulating, however. On the way there, she rehearses client presentations. On the way home, she attends to lingering emergencies and emails. Before and after, she comes up with new ideas. Many Parisians use the city's streets as a sort of creative gateway.

"My obsession with green began with the kitchen wall. This color is called 'Aqua Marine Deep.' Then came the fridge, the ottoman on the balcony, the blanket on the deck chair, the coffee mugs, the sugar bowl, and so on. It became a fixation. It's no longer the usefulness of the objects that counts, but the harmonious effect they produce."

"I settle in here to scan the Internet for inspiring conferences: Summit in Los Angeles, Fast Company in New York, House of Beautiful Business in Lisbon. Chimamanda Ngozi Adichie's TED conference is the video I've shared the most. She's an exceptional storyteller."

"The lightbulbs are bare because we never got around to installing the vintage light shades we found at the flea market. They've been in the closet for three years. We want to feel free to start all over again somewhere else."

"My place is filled with books. But I keep my favorites in the bathroom. Seeing them in the morning gets the ideas flowing. Flipping through them in the evening relaxes me. What am I reading now? A Distant Neighborhood *by Jirô Taniguchi and* The World According to Garp *by John Irving, which are stacked next to my micellar water."*

◀ *"My clothes rack, where I hang my prettiest garments. I bought the robe on the left just for display; I never wear it."*

"My coffee is ground and roasted in Paris, in Belleville. I buy it at Ten Belles, just downstairs on rue de la Grange-aux-Belles."

"If my vinyl record case caught fire, I'd save The Fleet Foxes' Helplessness Blues, *which includes my favorite song, 'Mykonos.' It's the perfect song for staring out the window of the bus, the metro, or the train and daydreaming."*

"I'm super-proud of the special edition on the city of tomorrow that we cowrote with Courrier International. *The city has been My Little Paris's playground for the last ten years. It encourages you to consider its future and invent new spaces—like the Book and Bed hostel I discovered in Tokyo, a library-hotel where the beds are arranged between the bookstacks!"*

JEAN-NICOLAS
Founder of the Billot Club

JULES JOFFRIN

He looks like any other twenty-six-year-old guy. But he's not really like any other twenty-six-year-old guy. Jean-Nicolas was sales director for Merci Alfred but dropped everything to become a butcher.

He's kind of the boss around his apartment. He moved in three years ago with three friends. They've since moved on, but others have taken their place. Jean-Nicolas has first say when it comes to hallway storage space. This arrangement doesn't stretch to the bedrooms, however: he occupies the smallest one in the apartment, in which he's managed to fit a cable-drum-cum-table and a coffee bag, the result of heated bargaining in Guatemala, which has since become a large cushion. Upcycled objects lend a certain *je ne sais quoi* to the living room: the Tikki-style bar, for instance, was found on page twenty-five of the online classifieds site Le Bon Coin and picked up from a funeral home. Objects are given a new lease on life, while the occupants here live life at full throttle.

"The game console is banned from the living room.
It's an area reserved for talking. We don't go there
to zone out in front of a screen. The best spot in
the apartment is the couch. It's so comfortable,
you could die of happiness just lying there. About
once every three months, we throw a big party
in the living room. We clear everything out,
put down a tarp, and bring in eighty people."

"We rescued this mask from a classified ad buried on a website. There's no real secret to finding little gems: you just have to dig deeper than everyone else. We made it our stability totem. Whoever has the most stable relationship with a girl gets to keep the totem in his room. The totem tends to rotate quite a bit, which is reassuring when you're not in a stable relationship."

"Vinyl is 'slow' music: another way of listening, involving movement and ceremony."

◀ *"Typically each of us has a set number of shoes in the hallway, except that I take up all the space. There are four shoe racks and four coat hangers and I take up three-quarters of them. In the mornings, between the toilet and the two bathrooms, this place turns into Place de Clichy. Everyone takes turns in the shower, including girlfriends or one-night stands— it gets pretty rock 'n' roll!"*

MARIE
Editor in Chief

—

RUE DES MARTYRS

Marie is constantly on the lookout. For the last seven years, she's been on the hunt for just the right words for My Little Paris newsletters, unearthing new spots that readers of My Little Kids will love and finding that perfect idea that will inspire subscribers to My Little Wedding. Amid all this activity, she also finds enough time to write children's books and to volunteer in hospitals. To recharge her creative batteries, she turns to her role model, Dr. Seuss. Little known in France but a cult favorite in the United States, this author knew exactly how to pen books that both parents and children devour with glee.

Marie's apartment is like her writing: filled with small details that make all the difference. The shelf near the fireplace is home to a mini-forest of pine trees brought back from the Vosges mountains. The bookshelf consists of wooden cubes mounted on the wall. She uses them to show off her favorite books, but also books she's written as gifts for friends and family. The cat purrs all day long on the couch, a reminder that all is well. In the kitchen, a stack of bowls painted with the family's first names hints at tenderness. Life should be filled with poetry. And Marie knows all the right words.

Flevy Frenchie

"Our apartment is rather small and oddly shaped.
It feels like a hut. And since we're on the sixth floor,
Bastien, my son, often says we live 'at the top of the tree,'
which feels appropriate."

"When Bastien was born, Nico and I repainted his room, hung frames on the wall, decorated. Now that he's here, the space belongs to him. It's his blank canvas. He arranges his stuffed animals, organizes his little cars—he's completely free to do what he wants. For example, he painted his box fort, gave it windows, and sometimes turns it into a garage. I wanted him to have the freedom to invent his own games. Stories have more weight when they come from within. We've been cultivating his imagination since he was a baby: his library has more books in it than ours. It's a point of pride."

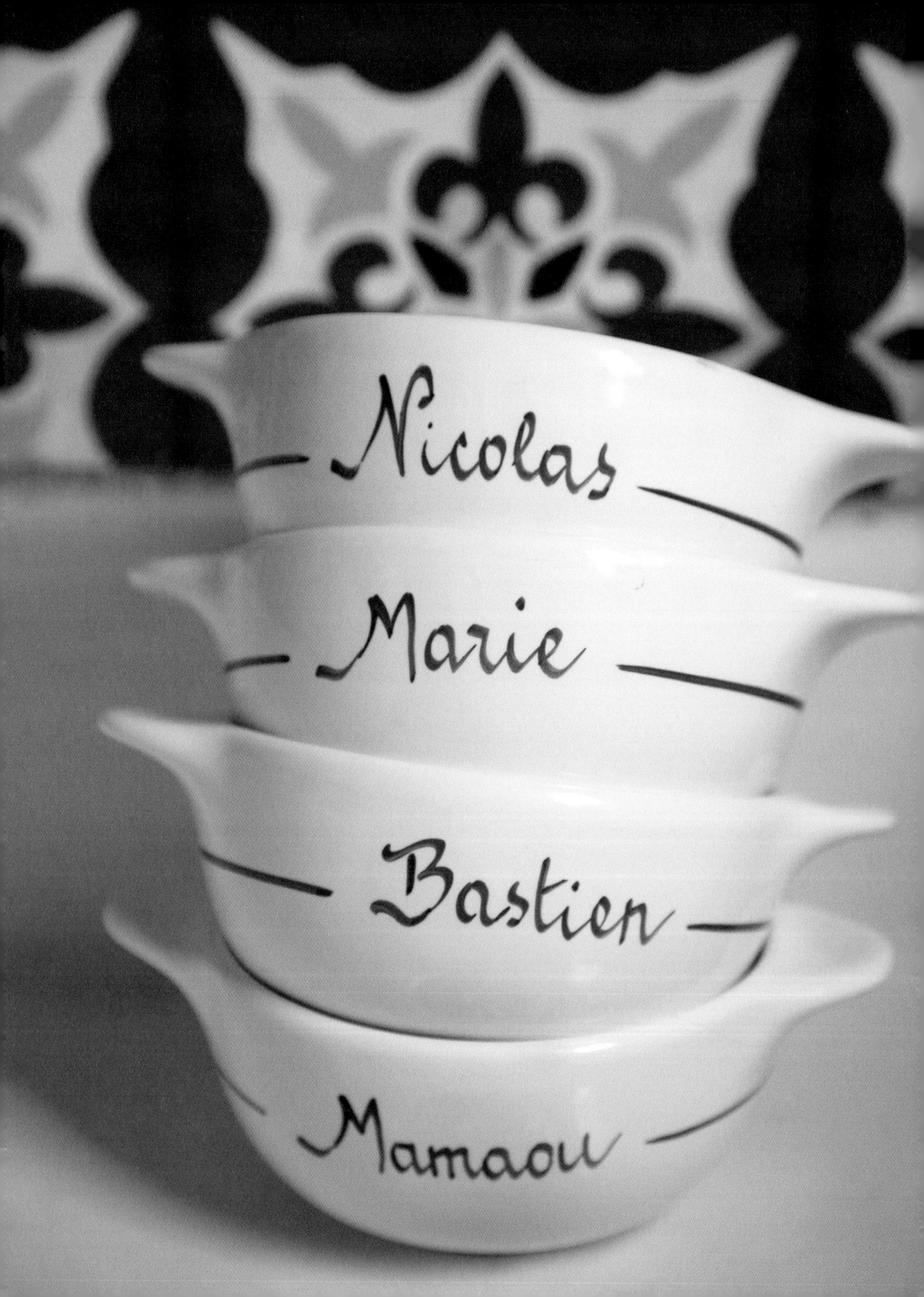
Nicolas
Marie
Bastien
Mamaou

"We have a ritual at My Little Paris: every year, we write our Culture Book. The book looks back on everything that's happened over the past year, from Friday cocktails to new business launches. We take photos of everything. I've worked on several of them, so for my five-year anniversary at My Little Paris I made my own Culture Book. I gave it to the twelve people who were there when I joined the company. That's when I realized how much we'd grown."

"I call them 'my oldies,' a bunch of old family photos. They're here for two reasons: as a reminder of unbelievable nineties fashions and, more importantly, of wonderful memories. Our elders watch over us. It's my 'Lion King' side, like when the king appears in the stars and says to Simba, 'Don't forget who you are.' We're fans of that Disney movie."

"My favorite season is when my mother gets out her huge copper jam pan. When I was a little girl, we'd spend afternoons together with my grandmother, removing pit after pit. I haven't bought jam since moving to Paris, it's a cardinal rule."

"This cat is the very image of stability. Whatever happens, whatever comes to pass, Metz (that's her name, and the city where I was born) will be purring on the couch. It's reassuring. In fact, she's the real resident in our apartment; she spends all her days here. If you think about it, it's her home we're living in."

DELPHINE

Product Development Manager

LEDRU-ROLLIN

What are Delphine's secret weapons? Scissors, tweezers, and . . . a crystal ball. In addition to making her own jewelry, she needs to predict the objects and accessories that are likely to delight My Little Box subscribers nine months down the line.

That ability to look ahead is a real talent. Delphine's apartment, for example, is just temporary. As a student, she lived in Bordeaux and Grenoble, where it was easy to find large apartments to share with roommates that she could furnish as she liked. In Paris, while she's waiting for the place of her dreams to show up, she's transformed a small studio into a workshop-cocoon perched high above the neighborhood. The furniture she's uncovered at flea markets, however, is waiting patiently at her parents' house.

"Last year, I spotted some earrings I liked on Instagram. I thought to myself, really, they look easy enough to make. So I bought some supplies. I started with two or three pieces, and then I went wild. Now I make earrings, jewelry. I'm even thinking about starting my own online store. I have lots of sketchbooks filled with designs just waiting to see the light of day."

"These cushion covers are from Indonesia, Thailand, and China. The handcrafted covers give my mini-balcony a bazaar-like vibe. They go well with the My Little Box Tokyo that I created, wrapped in its furoshiki— fabrics that are folded like origami and used to wrap gifts in Japan."

"I love vintage packaging. It conjures up other lives. The objects that wind up here need to have had a past. I collected a bunch of crates at the Marché d'Aligre, next door, so that I could organize my shoes."

"I love bringing baskets back from my travels. I came home from Morocco with four!"

PAULINE

Founder of Fripes Ketchup

—

LA CHAPELLE

The best antique dealers possess a special quality: a sixth sense that prompts them to dig around in boxes that everyone else walks right by, and to spot the corner of a frame that hints at a stunning painting or the damaged foot that turns out to belong to a beautiful armchair. You could also call it intuition. Pauline, the founder of a vintage store, has no shortage of it, as one glimpse at her apartment will confirm.

Parisian apartments are like advertisements in the metro: if you scratch away at a poster, you'll find older layers beneath, a tapestry of different colors, textures, and eras. Hiding under her white walls, Pauline found brick, wood, and wainscoting. And then left everything exactly as it was. She didn't decorate her apartment so much as unveil it.

*"Above my bed, I hung a collection
of paintings that I found in flea
markets, paintings that cost next
to nothing. My boyfriend and I call
them our 'romantic daubs.'"*

*"This kitchen sees a lot of use.
But not by me! I'm like Carrie
Bradshaw: 'My kitchen? I don't
even know where it is!'"*

*"When I started renovating my place,
I wanted to open it up first.
That's when I discovered the wood
beams and brick walls ... beautiful
materials that I wanted to showcase."*

"Luckily I'm a regular host of swap meets, because my closet is overflowing. As far as clothes go, I manage to stay reasonable. Things get a little out of hand when it comes to shoes, however. Because there isn't much space, I have to store my most beautiful pairs in pretty hard-to-reach places, so I never wear them."

"The bead necklaces are the only things in this apartment that I made myself—though the final look leaves a lot to be desired!"

"This fake cheese platter reminds me when to stop. Too much cheese, too much charcuterie, too many cocktails...."

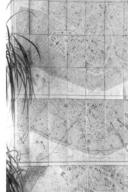

"At heart, I'm a fan of illustration, but I'm not as well versed in traditional art forms. So whenever I have the chance, I browse the flea markets for engravings. It's a way of educating myself."

JULIA

Founder of GoodMoods

—

RUEIL-MALMAISON

Julia has been steeped in colorful, stylish interiors since she was a little girl. But it was during her pregnancy, when she found herself confined at home earlier than planned, that she came up with the idea for GoodMoods: themed online moodboards showcasing chic products and telling readers where to buy them online. Julia combs through all the magazines, scrolls every website, and rummages through every flea market. In addition, each month she produces a selection of objects she has unearthed in antiques markets and customized by hand.

Like any good Parisian, Julia was hesitant about crossing the beltway—the Périphérique—that separates the city from the suburbs. Her husband held out longer than she did: during their first visit to see a house in the back of beyond, he arrived on his scooter, took off his helmet, declared, "Not on my life," and left as quickly as he had arrived. They hadn't counted on this former Napoleonic hunting lodge, however, which enticed them to take the leap. Julia successfully transformed the space without resorting to major renovations, using just a few well-chosen licks of paint. She has no regrets.

"The living room brings together all my favorite colors: gold, violet, evergreen, rust. There's a coffee table by the designer Charlotte Perriand in the center of the room, one originally created in 1962 but produced on a commercial basis for the first time in 2015. Whether I'm planning interiors for My Little Paris houses or twelve-bedroom Norman châteaux, daring to use color and unearthing rarities are a proven formula."

"My treasure shelves, my memory cabinets. I collect things, a little like Robert Saint-Cricq, a mid-century French artist who assembled and painted objects he found in the street (I have one of his works). One of my latest acquisitions is by André Sornay, a relatively unknown designer from the 1950s but someone who's attracting more interest now."

"I personalized the bathroom as much as I could, choosing this very graphic flooring from Bisazza (the design is by India Mahdavi, whom I really love) and, most importantly, a bathtub for cozy winter evenings in the country."

*"Manon, my eleven-year-old daughter,
gave me permission to go wild with the
colors in her room. Mission accomplished."*

"This is Léon's room, he's four. Color, lots of it. I particularly like the little chairs by French designer Jean-Louis Avril, who pioneered the creation of lacquered cardboard furniture in the 1960s."

"This poster is the first one I ever found on a classifieds site in Hawaii. It's a relic, basically!"

"This lamp is one I just designed. It's inspired by streetlamps in Paris. Along with the swing seat, it fills the garden with memories of childhood."

MARGOT

Experience Manager

—

MONTMARTRE

Two hundred fifty: that's how many dives Margot has under her belt. Perhaps that's why diving into the unknown doesn't scare her. She's in charge of conceiving and masterminding unique, one-of-a-kind events, and thousands of Parisians have enjoyed the ephemeral spaces she has invented. To keep her ideas fresh, she follows a morning ritual by reading her favorite marketing and digital innovation newsletter—ADN.

Margot is a little like a real-life Amélie Poulain. She was born, grew up, and almost always lived on rue Lepic, in Montmartre. But when she found a place with her husband, Stéphane, she agreed to leave her native soil for the other side of the hill, not so very far away. They chose this apartment for the two living-room windows that look out over the trees, making you feel like you're in the middle of a forest. Inside, however, the houseplants all died a year and a half ago—which she finds ironic.

"I love going to flea markets. I grab whole boxes that then disappear into the basement. At the same time my home remains spartan and very minimalist. I can't even bring myself to drill holes in the wall. It's a symptom of what I call 'Parisian schizophrenia!'"

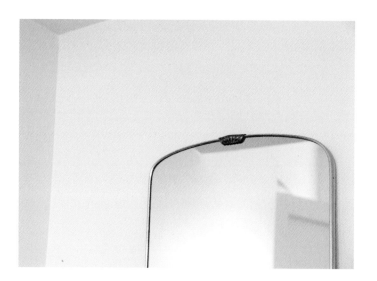

"All the photos on the rotating stand are our happiest memories. I like to have them close to me. When I was a little girl, I loved it when my parents told me about their memories. The time I fell down in the snow, the time I said something silly, and so on. It was always the same stories, but it was a kind of ritual. I've kept that. I'm very much into rituals and habits. I hate change."

"This is a vintage school map. I found it in a flea market in Montmartre. But I can't bring myself to hang it up. It's hell trying to make design choices in my house."

"Stéphane found this shell on the beach in Mexico. He hid my engagement ring inside it just before he proposed."

"This is the country-style pâté my grandmother makes. We call it Orville Pâté. (Orville is a tiny little village in the Loiret with just two houses.) It's become a cult foodstuff among our friends. They ask us to bring some back every time we visit her. My cousins and I wanted Grandma to become an entrepreneur and launch her own pâté start-up."

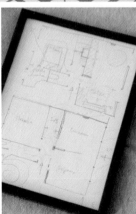

"When we bought our apartment, we celebrated with some friends. That night, we scribbled them a quick before/after sketch to show them the renovations we wanted to do. And when they came over for a drink about a year later, they gave it to us as a gift! This one I did hang up."

FANNY
Director of The School of Life

—

ABBESSES

Like her cats, Fanny can claim to have had nine lives. The first she spent traveling between France and Dubai wearing the high heels of a marketing director. In her latest incarnation, she donned a director's jacket to run The School of Life Paris. This life-skills institution, which originated in England, offers classes on all the stuff you don't learn in school: how to find the job of your dreams, how to boost creativity, and so on. Alongside her job, Fanny wrote a book, *Trêve de Bavardages: Retrouvons le goût de la conversation* (Enough Idle Chatter: Reviving the Art of Conversation), inspired by her own classes. And in addition to all that, she inspires My Little Paris with her off-the-wall ideas and tales of the new talents she meets.

Fanny is surrounded by souvenirs from her numerous lives. Against one wall is a chest of drawers from Bali, discovered at a Greek antique dealer's shop in Dubai (are you following?). Next to that, her great-grandfather's card table. One day, she stumbled upon a secret drawer; inside were the playing cards that had cost her ancestor his entire fortune. She smiles. Her own most precious possessions are the old letters she keeps in her letter chest.

"My 'Her' chair by Fabio Novembre. The cheeky nature of Italian design makes me want to hunt for vintage objects."

"I buy my eggshell porcelain teacups at flea markets for next to nothing, though they're actually worth a fortune. Because they're extraordinarily fine they're all slightly chipped. I find the little cracks touching."

*"One of my morning rituals is   ▶
doing yoga on my balcony.
I call it the 'Salutation
to the Sacré-Coeur'!"*

"I went to a cocktail class at the Hemingway Bar at the Ritz. The barman, Colin Field, doesn't really teach you how to make cocktails, but he does reveal the secrets of that famous Parisian hotel, which is even better. At the end of the class, he offered us a glass of champagne. Do you know the legend about the first champagne glass? Supposedly it was molded from the breast of the Marquise de Pompadour. Guess what: the ones at the Ritz fit me perfectly!"

"There's a story behind my Syrian trunk-closet, which I found at a flea market in Luxembourg. It came from a château estate sale. When I cleaned it, I discovered a little label inside with the name and address of the manufacturer in Syria. Several months later, when I was in Syria, I found the craftsman's street. The store had closed, but I love the idea of having gone back to its roots."

CHARLES

Antiques Dealer
Founder of Tombées du Camion

SAINT-DENIS

A Sunday in spring. The day before, you heard about an antiques market nearby. You show up in the morning, around nine o'clock, feeling optimistic and hoping to find some treasures. But when you arrive, the great finds are already long gone, carted off in a truck belonging to a professional antiques dealer like Charles. These are the kind of spoils that Charles sells in Tombées du Camion, a store in the Saint-Ouen flea market that is also a veritable Aladdin's cave of quirky objects.

Charles used to mock homebodies who spent all their time indoors, never taking advantage of Paris. But then he bought this place, which he intended to use as a stockroom: there was plenty of space, including a garage, and it was easy to get to from the flea market. Then, after mulling the idea over for some time, he decided to move in, but only after setting himself a challenge: that of avoiding, at all costs, the look of the typical "antique dealer's house"—that hotchpotch cliché of objects strewn everywhere. But for the first time in his life Charles finally had enough space to decorate his home with the objects he loves. He caved in, of course.

"Since I hadn't intended to display any objects to begin with, I wanted to keep the walls unfinished, thinking, 'It will be decorative.' For starters, it saved me at least two months of renovation. And ultimately, it's also very beautiful."

*"The real luxury here is this courtyard,
a little slice of the country just a
stone's throw from Paris. For our
housewarming party, we set up
a table for fifty people between
the garage and the courtyard."*

*"The house used to belong to
some Evangelists. They'd set up
a chapel in the garage. Since I have
a kind of fascination with funerary
objects, you could say that a certain
continuity has been respected."*

Ce film retrace l'histoire
d'un de ces hommes et de
la jeune fille qu'il rencontra
un jour par hasard.

"We came across this authentic zinc countertop—rare because it didn't contain holes for a beer tap. We rebuilt the bar underneath. It helps break up the space, like the platform in the living room. I don't like too many walls; everything is open here."

"*I like to repurpose the religious objects I find in flea markets. For example, the cross hanging upside-down is just for turning my lamp on or off, there's nothing satanic about it. That being said, there's a connection: 'Where there is light, there is darkness.' The sign 'God sees me' is painted on glass and once presided over a monastery. In my house, it's obviously less frightening!*"

"*My vanities: these three skulls are all that's left of the Three Graces.*"

"*This is my Sunday barbecue: I serve tuna and swordfish with red peppers and sliced zucchini slathered in olive oil. It wouldn't be anything special if it weren't washed down with a few restorative bottles of red wine.*"

◀ "*Objects have no meaning other than the one we give them. This little mannequin is an ode to half-formed artists like myself.*"

USHA
Founder of Jamini

PASSAGE BRADY

Usha is a former L'Oréal employee whose Northeast Indian heritage caught up with her when she founded the brand Jamini. Her specialty is matching the traditional skills of craftspeople from the Assam region of India with Parisian taste in homewares. Usha cares about the villages she works with: she wanted more than just getting products to market, she wanted to create a network that would support local weavers. It's this human touch that makes her collections all the more appealing.

What's the point of traveling around the world if you end up surrounded by objects you could have found anywhere? To earn a place in Usha's apartment, items must fulfill two conditions: they must be unique, and they must have a story to tell. An old Afghan rug, Scandinavian furniture, and a basket from Assam all passed the test. However, Usha likes to vary her decor: textiles, photos—everything changes regularly. According to her, the smaller a space is, the less it should be left alone.

"Working with fabric is a little like cooking: when you know how to cook, you can improvise, and it will always taste good. The same goes for my cushions: I never studied design, but I follow my instincts when it comes to choosing materials and colors."

"I think I became an entrepreneur because I enjoy the taste of freedom. I have a hard time following orders. Design is the same: there's not just one style, but many different styles to choose from."

"Claudio, my partner, is a photographer (he exhibited at the Venice Biennale). Elisa, my daughter, likes to draw. We all have our own means of artistic expression, so we give ourselves a little exhibition space on our own walls."

"I bring a lot of jewelry back from my travels but I don't want to sell it just now. When you're an entrepreneur, you are sometimes tempted to turn everything into a business. You have to learn to resist."

"This boar is one of the seven avatars of Vishnu, the protector of the Hindu trinity. The animal and the human are closely intertwined in Hindu mythology. This connection can be found in the patterns of certain textiles."

MARION
Chef and Cake-Maker

—

JAURÈS

Marion is the resident chef at My Little Paris. To feed her colleagues, entertain clients, and just for the fun of it, every day she cooks up a storm in the start-up's offices. These meals have the habit of turning into multi-course lunches, where outstanding dishes are served on flea-market china. Messages and ideas somehow flow more easily when everyone is enjoying a good meal, elbows on the table. Many My Little Paris projects have crystallized over dessert. What's Marion's secret for helping clinch the deal? Apricots roasted with thyme and topped with freshly whipped cream.

Her kitchen at home is just as special, as you'd expect. Marion stocks and organizes her fridge with military precision. She has a drawer filled with an impressive array of little labeled jars containing seeds and oils. She's wild about spices. She takes an entire crate with her when she cooks for private clients or at events. She also bakes a mean madeleine, just one of the meltingly soft cakes she produces under the nickname "Mademoiselle Proust." Did we mention that she cooks the best roast chicken in Paris? Simply put, your mouth is always watering when Marion's around.

"I eat a lot of vegetables seasoned
with all kinds of spices and Asian
condiments. My fridge looks like a
laboratory because I keep quite a
few essential oils in little test tubes.
I use them a lot for cooking and as
natural remedies."

"'Appetite comes with eating. Thirst is quenched by drinking.' Rabelais totally had the right idea."

*"I inherited the dressing table from ▶
my great-grandfather. It hasn't
left my room since it arrived. No
matter what apartment I'm living
in, this old piece of furniture gives
it instant style. It's important to
have at least one piece of furniture
older than you in your home."*

"This bar of chocolate weighs over two pounds! It's my biggest guilty pleasure."

"There are works of literature strewn among the cookbooks. Appreciating good things and good words is not so different at the end of the day."

"This is my first collection of pastry recipes. My two grandmothers gave it to me when I was six or seven years old. They wrote all the recipes. I'm never without it."

"I found this collection of earthenware knife rests at a flea market in the Cévennes at least ten years ago. I'm the daughter of an antiques dealer; I caught the bug early."

CLÉMENCE

Artistic Director

PIGALLE

The poster in the living room joyfully declares that "Beauty will save the world." Clémence has made it her motto. Her job is to give shape and color to every project she's involved in. Whether she's designing a website that will be looked at for several minutes or an apartment that will be lived in for several years, the same rule applies: you have to make people want to stay as long as possible.

When she bought this place, Clémence decided to redo it from top to bottom. She tore down walls and changed the ceiling, looking to start with a fresh slate. Being a fan of illustration, she quickly added a few touches of color. And many, many pairs of sneakers: Clémence always has a yoga class or a marathon workout to get to.

"We met the street artists Toqué Frères through a friend. We liked their work so we bought this poster that's been propped up in the kitchen ever since."

"It took me a while to get my boyfriend interested in sports. I managed to do it by sitting him down in front of Lucile Woodward's videos. She's an incredible fitness coach and she's very good at motivating people."

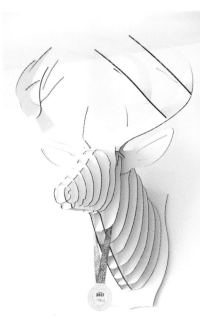

"Since I started running, I've collected quite a few medals, but my best memory is still my first marathon. I didn't tell anyone I was training for it. For three months, I felt as if I were leading a double life. The first thing I did when I crossed the finish line was to call my dad; he was blown away."

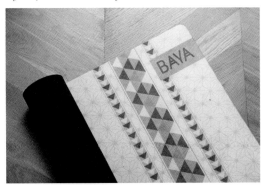

"I collect the **Alice** series of books for young adults. I found the first volume in my grandmother's attic when I was nine years old. Now I have more than five hundred. Some date back to the 1950s, and some are even in Danish."

"I'm crazy about Virginie Morgand's work. She often drew divers, swimmers, and dancers. I recently discovered that she even designed posters for the London Underground. She's brought my walls to life."

"I love this doormat and the idea of finding a nice message when you come home."

ÉMILE
Artistic Director

—

JULES JOFFRIN

Émile spends his time drawing, converting, retouching, and formatting. He also creates backdrops for pop-up restaurants and publicity campaigns that cover the streets of Paris. He develops his own photos, of course. And he is continually redoing his apartment … as you might expect.

Nothing is final chez Émile. The lamps from his former apartment still haven't been installed. And he owns some rare frames that will hang on the wall one day. He lives in the eighteenth arrondissement, where some people have retained the customs of times gone by. When he moved in, the apartment's owner asked Émile how much he wanted to pay. They came to an agreement, then shook hands. This is the only contract they've ever had.

(Preceding pages)
*"What I like most about this room are
the blinds. I think they've been there
for at least thirty years. When I take
a nap on the weekends, the light filters
in and dapples the facing wall. It makes
for a very calming ambience."*

"As often happens in Parisian apartments, when I throw parties people rarely gather in the living room but seem to prefer spaces like the hallway or my kitchen. And sometimes that takes its toll. This mark, which I decided to call a 'galaxy', reminds me that one of my buddies nearly started a fire here."

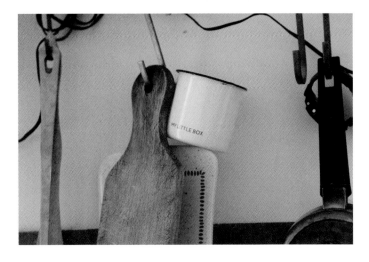

"I buy 45s in lots at stock sales. Then I invite friends over and we listen to them at random. We discover some fun stuff. They're also a source of graphic inspiration."

"This zigzag bottle opener belonged to my great-grandfather. It's only the best bottle opener in the world: you tighten, you pull … and that's it."

"What I'm most proud of about this camera collection is that they all work, even the one from 1917."

"I hid my wardrobe behind a camouflage net I bought at the flea market; you can get them for next to nothing."

ANNE-FLORE
Cofounder of My Little Paris

—

MONTMARTRE

Anne-Flore used to like collecting things: diplomas and degrees from prestigious Parisian schools; a teaching certificate in geography. Jobs: professor, in-house lawyer, cemetery caretaker. In 2008, she dropped it all and started My Little Paris. Since then, she's been an editor, a project starter, a napkin brainstormer, and a general director. For ten years now, she's lived her life in step with the start-up. And the larger the group grows, the more important it is not to forget the smaller details. Anne-Flore keeps them in mind by reading Daniel Arasse's essays on art history, *On n'y voit rien* (We See Nothing There) and *Le Détail* (The Detail). She shares the same motto as My Little Paris: "Little things make big differences."

Anne-Flore never liked Montmartre. Montmartre is Paris for tourists. And yet she moved here three years ago, right into the same apartment that her husband's uncle occupied in the 1970s. It was pure coincidence; they took it as a sign, though from whom isn't clear. In the mornings, they wake to the sound of the bells. At night, when their windows are open, it's not uncommon to hear music drifting out. If Paris never sleeps, it's partly their fault.

FRANÇOIS NARS

◀ *"We never read the illustrated books we buy, it's a bit of a shame. Half my bookcase is exhibition catalogs. I haven't seen all the exhibitions, but I like opening them at random just for a break. Which one is currently on the go? Dries Van Noten at the Musée des Arts Décoratifs: he thinks that routine kills inspiration, as his collections make clear. The couch is like an ocean liner. Once you're on it, you sail out the window, into the Parisian sky, over the gardens of the Musée de Montmartre, and all the way to La Défense."*

"At 7 a.m., when there's no one in Montmartre, the Sacré-Coeur is the most beautiful place in the city. In the evening, despite having to climb three hundred steps, it's nice coming home to this peaceful hillside. It almost feels as if the place is relieved that all the tourists have cleared out. Last year we opened the My Little Paris Maison de Montmartre, a slow office space for reflecting on new projects that also hosts our Tokyo and Berlin teams. It was located just next door on Allée des Brouillards. I never left Montmartre after that."

"We lightened the hardwood floors everywhere, and in the bedroom the floor is actually white, Swedish-style. The winters are long up there; it provides a dose of summer and light."

"I discovered this screen in Chatou, during the Ham and Antiques Festival (it sounds weird, but it's a very well-regarded event). I thought it was wonderful, but I had no use for it. In the end, I turned it on its side and made it into a headboard."

◄ *"Alex wore this Scots Guard uniform when we were (re)married in Las Vegas, just after buying it at a thrift store in Los Angeles. The ties are made by his brand, Cinabre. Everything is made in France; he even supplies Emmanuel Macron."*

"The couch is a recent arrival. I had several sets of cushion covers made so that I can change them with the seasons. It's a serious business."

"Our cupboards are overflowing with dishware gleaned from flea markets. It's my thing when I go bargain hunting. For our wedding, I spent a year collecting six hundred mismatched plates from all over France."

"There are always boxes of Monaco in the cocktail cupboard—it's an essential."

"My collection of nineties T-shirts features all the iconic television shows: Dallas, Dynasty, Beverly Hills, Love Boat, *and so on. They're brilliant ice-breakers at parties. It's much better to talk about something that isn't work-related. It makes for more interesting conversations."*

MAEVA AND SIBYLLE

*Partnership Manager
and Brand Manager*

PASSAGE BRADY

They live together and they work together, but they have a rule: no talking shop at home. Sibylle is in charge of growing the My Little Box brand, while Maeva oversees partnerships and the cosmetics that make their way into the box. The only time they touch on work is when they share the latest innovations they've spotted on Racked or Refinery29, their favorite online references.

They ended up in their apartment on a whim. Sibylle was the only woman in an otherwise all-male apartment share, and Maeva had been living in the same place for six years. Within six days, they'd packed their bags and settled down near Passage Brady. Three girls now share the apartment; it's bustling and full of life.

"This is a party neighborhood. We host a lot of parties, but the neighbors have never said anything. Most of them have been here more than twenty years. They've become immune. When we have people over, one of us picks up the necessaries at the Lebanese restaurant downstairs, and the other heads to the wine shop."

"What's nice about being in an all-girl apartment share is that we each sort of have three closets. We pick things out here and there, we mix it up!"

"We brought this vase back from a trip to Morocco. It was our first real 'design object.' Our friends came back with tons of jewelry and we came back with a vase. We were the weirdos in the group."

"We rarely cook meals ourselves, but we do love eating. Sardines brought back from Lisbon are the best solution."

"A lot of tea-drinking goes on here. It's our after-dinner ritual. Often, when we don't eat together, we know we're going to meet up after. There's something very reassuring about it, like being part of a family."

CÉLINE
Cofounder of My Little Paris

—

LAMARCK

Céline likes to dream, but she's not the type do so on her own. Instead she inspires her teams to feats of imagination: visualizing the city of tomorrow on 2½ acres (1 hectare) of wasteland in northeast Paris; setting up a 500-seat table along the Seine River; giving women the means to accomplish their projects by launching the Mona community. She feeds this personal ambition by reading *Creative Visualization: Use the Power of Your Imagination to Create What You Want in Your Life* by Shakti Gawain—a "hippy book from the 1970s," as she describes it. That's where she got her conviction that the craziest ideas are the ones worth following.

After a childhood spent in Brittany, and a dozen moves between Paris, London, Dakar, Hong Kong, and Montreal, Céline arrived in Montmartre two years ago and moved into the kind of apartment she'd been dreaming of since she saw *The Aristocats* as a child. It has a quirky layout: the stove is behind the couch, and you have to walk through three rooms to get to the terrace, which hovers over a sea of Parisian rooftops. This apartment is also where her first daughter grew up. The second just joined the family.

*"When I started developing Mona, our coworking space for
women, my feminist credentials seemed pretty lightweight.
So I changed my entire library. I became completely obsessed
with the issue. For the last year, inspired by the Librairie des
Femmes (Women's Bookshop) on rue Jacob, the bastion of the
MLF (French Lay Mission), I soaked up Léonora Miano, Susan
Sontag, Chimamanda Ngozi Adichie, and so on. For my daughter,
I threw out* **Little Brown Bear** *in favor of* **Rose Bonbon** *by Adela
Turin, an absolutely brilliant feminist book from the 1970s. As
for the couch, it's in the process of becoming a podcast listening
station. But I also listen to Arte Radio,* **Quoi de Meufs** *(What's New
Ladies?),* **LSD,** *and* **Where Should We Begin?** *with Esther Perel."*

"My everyday life at My Little Paris is as ▶
*exciting as it is hectic. I like coming
home to design that doesn't make a sound.
And yet I also need cheerfulness. So
I placed little touches of color everywhere,
inside the cabinets. There should always be
a little color on hand in the cupboards."*

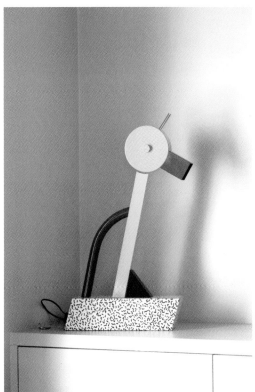

"*My dishware is a mixture of gifts, travel souvenirs, and objects found online. It's one of my addictions: I have phases where I can spend nights combing the classifieds. eBay is my Tinder.*"

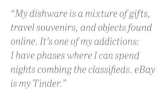

"Even before my eldest daughter, Mahaut, was born, I was interested in education. I try to support her need for independence, so her bed has no bars and it's at floor level. She's fallen out a few times, but now she just wakes up and gets on with things. She's gained in autonomy, and we've gained in longer sleep-ins."

"I grew up in Brittany and dreamed of Paris for years before moving. I have a voracious appetite for this city. Ten years later I still find it incredible to be living here. I found the view I'd been dreaming of from this balcony. Alex has set up a permaculture 'garden': the three strawberries we picked after two years of work were the best celebration ever."

"I'm addicted to tea. My favorite is Hojicha, for its slightly coppery taste. Ippodo's is the best. I bring a suitcase back with me when I go to Tokyo. In these quantities, it's almost contraband."

"In the evening, I have two rituals: reading poetry and reading cookbooks. Perla Servan-Schreiber's book is a wonderful combination of the two. It includes this quote from Dogen Zenji: 'A leader's function, regardless of his or her field, requires three qualities: a zest for life, kindness, and magnanimity.' I'd agree."

◄ "As a huge fan of Pixar, I love objects that look as if they might come to life. Like this jar: I wouldn't be surprised if it suddenly started to talk."

ENORA
Human Resources Manager

CHARONNE

Every new arrival at My Little Paris is given a book called *Delivering Happiness: A Path to Profits, Passion, and Purpose* by Tony Hsieh, CEO of clothing company Zappos. It's Enora's cult book; she received a copy the day she joined the company and had the idea of giving one to all newcomers. Eventually the new arrivals become old hands, of course, but they still turn to her. One hundred thirty employees equals one hundred thirty people longing to learn, innovate, and change: it's a huge, boisterous tribe to manage, but she knows how to do it.

Enora's apartment was a lucky find. She was visiting the one just downstairs but didn't like it and told the real-estate agent as much. He got the message and showed her this one instead. That was three years ago and, despite its small size, the bizarre bathroom layout, and lack of storage space, she wouldn't give it up for the world. Here, her heirloom place mats cohabit with the latest issue of *Harvard Business Review*. It's her cocoon.

"I created my own bubble of tranquility in 215 square feet (20 square meters). My egg chair is my favorite spot. I read in it, I tan in it. But, to be honest, I spent most of my time in bed. It's my living room, my dining room, and my office."

"You have to be incredibly resourceful when you don't have a closet. I store my underwear in wicker baskets— it's a very practical solution! I'm like the Marie Kondo of Paris: when I buy something, I force myself to get rid of something else."

*"The four foods
I can't do
without."*

*"I customized this piece myself.
It's a Parisian sideboard that was
manufactured between the two
world wars especially for Parisian
kitchens, which were smaller
than others. One day, on my way
back from Brittany, I picked it
up and brought it home. It's a
nice reflection of my life here."*

*"I love crocheted place mats.
I have lots, all of them
family heirlooms. My
grandmother made this one."*

PERLA
Author and Essayist

PARC MONCEAU

Sitting down and listening to Perla Servan-Schreiber talk is one of the little pleasures that the founders of My Little Paris can enjoy. She is happy to share her experiences of working as a publicist at *Elle* and *Marie Claire* in the 1970s and 1980s, the golden age of fashion magazines. It was there, under the watchful eye of photographers and designers, that Perla honed her taste for the beautiful. Then, with her husband Jean-Louis, she launched *Psychologies Magazine* and *Clés*. She followed up with a book about what life taught her—lessons that have left their mark on her stylish apartment in western Paris.

The doorway that connects her office to the kitchen is her favorite area. Cooking is essential for Perla. It's a time for meditation and for nourishing her inner life. It's also a way of taking care of others. She discovered the pleasures of cooking at age sixteen, when she moved out of her parents' home. She took some pots and pans and just started, she says. Her repertoire was very limited, but her desire to cook never waned. One of the great discoveries that comes with age is learning how to simplify one's life. That may be why Perla dresses only in white. It's gentle, calming. Unburdening yourself from objects, people, travel—this lesson is perhaps the most important one she has learned, as she explains in her book *Les Promesses de l'âge* (The Joys that Come with Age).

"I have a lot of rituals. Morning rituals like eating fruit, walking, meditation. Rituals before dinner, when I take the time to remove my makeup and take care of myself. My favorite ritual, I think, is afternoon tea. Jean-Louis and I don't eat lunch, so around 3.30 p.m. he starts pacing about because his stomach is rumbling. I always make little cakes for teatime, or something sweet."

"When I moved in, the kitchen was only a quarter of the size it is now. I tore everything down. This is my first real kitchen. During the renovations, a friend came by and suggested I cut a section out of the wall to connect my kitchen to my office via the dressing room. Since then, it's become a gateway of sorts."

"I love clothes. I've worn only white for the last thirty-five years. It doesn't feel like a choice. It's as if the color chose me. I've gone through two white phases. In between there was a colorful interlude when I met Romeo Gigli, an Italian couture designer who I adore and who does exceptional colors. One day he said, 'You must come to the studio.' Off I went to rue de Sévigné. He talked me into it, and thereafter I wore nothing except mustard, bronze.... That lasted for several years, and then I returned to the simplicity of white. It recharges my batteries, it calms me. Surrounded by essentials, that's when I'm at my happiest."

LE MEILLEUR & LE PLUS SIMPLE DE ROB

S,
"

Perla Servan-Schre

Desserts

Le
Bonheu
de
cuisiner

Servan-Schre

ATELIER SAVEURS

"If I had to choose only one thing from my apartment, it would be my ivory hairpin for my bun. And books by Etty Hillesum and Rainer Maria Rilke. **Letters to a Young Poet** *has underlining on every page.*"

"*This is the first chair Tom Dixon designed, and it's the first piece I bought for myself. I spent a fortune on it.*"

"*I never imagined having someone like Jean-Louis in my life. He had nothing in common with any of my previous fiancés, but when I saw him, I recognized him. Meeting someone is a jump into the unknown. Let yourself go, open your heart, open your arms, and give them everything.*"

◀ "**Le Bonheur de Cuisiner** (*The Happiness of Cooking*) *was my first cookbook. I spent two years sorting, honing, adjusting, and rewriting each recipe. I also included my grandchildren's favorite desserts: Léon's cake, Pénélope's mousse, crêpes for Luc.*"

MARIE
Creative Planner

—

CONDORCET

Marie's role is to turn simple hunches into huge projects and take ideas as far as they can go. She's always subscribed to the idea that creativity is a muscle that needs to be exercised everyday, and regularly turns to *Creativity Inc.*, by Ed Catmull, the co-founder of Pixar, for inspiration. It's the work that's had the greatest influence on her.

Marie and Victor left their apartment bare for a long time. It was their first, and they didn't want to rush the decor, so they waited patiently before furnishing it and bringing it to life. On the weekends, Victor coopts the living-room table as his workshop. He's been a cabinetmaker since he was six years old and used to build forts in his parents' garden, but these days turntable stands and stylish lamp bases are more his thing. Woodworking is like planning a project, after all: the journey from sketch to final result is exactly the same.

"I like saying we 'craft our dreams,' because in a way it's true. We spent a long time looking for a TV unit with enough room for the turntable and space to store our records. We never found it, so Victor made one. I dream of having a dining-room table like the ones in interior design magazines, with strips of leather on the corners and distressed wood. It's our next project."

"Most of the furniture in the apartment is handmade by Victor. It's truly custom-made, so there are errors and imperfections in almost every object. At first, I didn't like the flaws: they were all I saw. I still notice them, but now they're the parts I like best."

"Surf Shack, a Californian design magazine, is my reference manual for my dream house: wood, handcrafted furniture, surf … it's got it all."

"These seats are completely upcycled. Victor attached discs of wood from his parents' garden to simple stool bases from Ikea."

"Every time I have friends over, I take pictures of them with our Polaroid. It's the guest Polaroid; it stays in the living room. I like having souvenirs of everyday life."

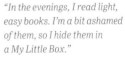

"In the evenings, I read light, easy books. I'm a bit ashamed of them, so I hide them in a My Little Box."

"I really like plants, but the feeling's not mutual."

FANY
Serial Entrepreneur

HÔTEL DE VILLE

The founder of My Little Paris, Fany now oversees the cosmetics brand Seasonly. She comes up with a thousand ideas a second. She likes the energy of new beginnings, working miracles with next to nothing, and the excitement of the unknown. Fany is one of those passionate people driven by their entrepreneurial nature. What's the book on her bedside table? *The Business Romantic* by Tim Leberecht. Her personal motto? It's better to try something quickly than spend a long time thinking about it.

This is exactly the philosophy she followed when she decorated her apartment. She doesn't care so much about the neighborhood: it's Paris she loves. Period. She wanted a space where she could shake things up. She loves entertaining friends downstairs, but upstairs is her sanctuary. Here she ignores the rules of interior design and all the latest trends, concentrating instead on the things she likes. So her pizza oven, her desk, and her bathtub rub shoulders high above the city. Up here, under the eaves, she's created her own version of *Eat, Pray, Love*.

*"When I moved in, I tore everything down.
The remodeling took only two months. I played
site foreman: I showed up every day to oversee the
workers. Upstairs, there were three bedrooms, but
I turned them into one large room. Because I don't
really like clothes, I asked them to make me a
walk-in closet like a fisherman's cabin, to
encourage me to actually use it."*

*"I love charcuterie. I even did
a 'pâté and dried sausage'
workshop. And I love cooking
in general. I have lots of cookbooks and
spices. The white paint and wooden
shelves give the kitchen a kind
of American vacation-home feel."*

"Why did I put plants on the staircase? To block it off, obviously! Upstairs is my space; I want to keep it that way. Plants are a good way of doing just that. No one wants to step over a plant."

"With a calzone on my plate and the
rooftops of Paris in the background,
this terrace is my idea of paradise.
I can't imagine anything better."

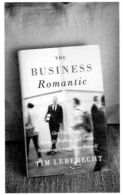

"In the mornings, I always start with the earrings. That's how I decide what I'm going to wear. I even made myself an earring closet."

*"My collection of **Fast Company** magazines. I'm a fan, but women are not featured on the cover often enough. That's gradually changing, however."*

"The shelf with the spices is the most important one in my kitchen. I never cook anything without spices: they add that final touch that makes all the difference."

CÉLINE
Chef

—

PETITES ÉCURIES

Céline Pham doesn't cook, she tells stories. Everything she knows, she learned from her Vietnamese grandmother who ran a restaurant. When she died, Céline quit her job in music and installed herself in the kitchens. Since then, she's been cooking on the move: six months at Fulgurances, the Parisian pop-up that changes chefs twice a year; a summer residency at a restaurant in Guéthary in the Basque Country; and candlelit dinners for private clients the rest of the time.

This apartment is the first Céline's settled down in. She shares it with Ulysse, a ginger tomcat—and quite possibly the best-fed feline in Paris. The large oak table is where it all happens. On Sundays, Céline hosts roast chicken dinners that last for hours—another of her grandmother's traditions—while, during the week, the table becomes an oversized worktop where friends put their heads together. Céline often says that Vietnamese people are emotionally autistic and convey their love through cooking. I think we've got the message.

*"When I moved in, the apartment was just an empty shell.
A very good friend went hunting for me and found all
the furniture at flea markets. It all fits perfectly into this
space, but if I ever leave I won't necessarily be able to take
everything with me."*

"My parents crossed paths here,
in the eighteenth arrondissement,
after they'd both arrived from Saigon.
My father then scoured all of Paris in
search of the woman he'd met ... and
eventually found her."

"I have two hundred knives in my drawers. Really, knives are weapons. I even have one that still had camel hair stuck to it when I bought it!"

"I love these matches. I bring back whole packets when I go to Vietnam."

"In Vietnam, food is the language of the heart."

"My dice are my lucky charms. I have one or two by Hermès. They symbolize chance and random encounters. Ulysse loves playing with them."

DIANE
Beekeeper on the Roofs of Paris

—

GRANDS BOULEVARDS

Diane left the verdant forests of Osnabrück in Germany for the grey rooftops of Paris thirty-six years ago. She's been a beekeeper for ten years. Normally she changes jobs every eight years, but beekeeping is one she stuck to, having dreamed of it since childhood.

Her hive is located on the roof where she lives. Her apartment was once a sunroom for dancers from the Folies Bergère: those ladies had allover tans. Now it's Diane's own dance hall, complete with paper lanterns, lounge chairs, and a small bedroom, perched on high, that she rents out from time to time. She's a creature of habit when it comes to the most beautiful sunset in Paris. She always turns up on time and sits in the same place, glass of wine in hand. When the sun disappears behind the Eiffel Tower, she turns her gaze toward the Sacré-Coeur. The lights come on; then it's time for her to go to bed.

"The entrance to the building isn't great because these days it's a parking lot. That always surprises visitors. In the 1930s, it was the first swimming pool in Paris. There was direct access to the sunroom, which was here. There were fitness rooms on the fifth and sixth floors. That's where famous circus artists used to train."

"The honey the bees produce is for
them, it's their winter reserves.
We're only allowed to take the surplus.
It wasn't a money-making enterprise
for me at the beginning, but then
I met someone who was setting up a
teaching hive in Normandy. Since then,
I've hosted beekeeping workshops
at my home, in my kitchen, and on
my terrace."

"The living room that opens onto the terrace is my adventurer's cabin. I've been lucky enough to live with the Papuan people in New Guinea, accompany researchers to Antarctica on an icebreaker, live in Indonesia for a year.... That's why I have so many pieces of furniture from elsewhere. This apartment is my refuge."

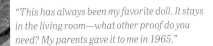

"This has always been my favorite doll. It stays in the living room—what other proof do you need? My parents gave it to me in 1965."

"The designer Alyssa Jos just created this plant-shaped pouf. It looks like it comes from some kind of imaginary forest. I love slipping between its petals and daydreaming until I drift off. That's what happiness feels like."

"This is the work of Guillaume Massé, an artist who belongs to the PannArt movement. He collects roadside objects like this one—signs, distance markers, and so on—cleans them up, and gives them funny little messages. It's a taste of the street transported to the Parisian rooftops."

AT WORK

PARIS

A Former Merry-Go-Round Factory

Up until the 1970s, Barbès in northern Paris was a theater
and entertainment district. Way back then, a rather unusual
building stood at number 13, boulevard de Rochechouart:
a factory where they made merry-go-rounds. Sculptors
carved the wooden horses, mechanics put the motorized
parts together, and engineers assured overall sturdiness.
Machines to sweep children off their feet were assembled
in the passageways. My Little Paris strives to keep this craft
tradition alive in the digital world.

A daily dose of creativity

Creativity is like a muscle: it needs to be exercised daily. In the My Little Paris offices, everyone has the opportunity to subscribe to mental jogging sessions: there are Creative Mornings, breakfasts with inspiring individuals; Zero Workshops, which help unleash the imagination; and Bistrot Debriefings, which offer a dive into international news with Fast Company, Wired, Monocle, *and similar publications. Everything takes place in the learning space carved out on the ground floor, on tiered, cushioned seating. The only creative ritual held outside the offices is the Megalab, an internal TED conference at a theater in Montmartre where, one by one, My Little collaborators take to the stage, microphone in hand, to share topics they've felt excited about during the previous month.*

Books, books everywhere

Every My Little Paris project addresses the digital realm: online media (Merci Alfred, Tapage, Mona, My Little Beauty, My Little Kids, etc.), start-up initiatives (Urban Lab), and international e-commerce brands (My Little Box, Gambettes Box, Gina). And yet the teams are fueled by the printed word: they have unlimited credit for buying as many books as they want, and books are given pride of place in the offices. On the top floor, a dedicated bookcase contains only life-changing titles—allowed into the office only after they've been read and approved by a member of the team. They include Noah Scalin's journal 365: A Daily Creative Journal: Make Something and Change Your Life, *Gretchen Rubin's* The Happiness Project, *and Catherine Taret's* Il n'est jamais trop tard pour éclore (Chronicles of a Late Bloomer).

The un-table

It doesn't take much to free yourself. Often it's just a matter of traveling light: a computer and a telephone are all that's needed to get the work done. In any case, it's better to avoid having too much stuff, so that you're free to migrate from one space to another, one neighbor to another, one job to another, from one day to the next. The My Little Paris offices meet what we call the "convergence criterion": spaces are arranged so as to invite movement, friction, and interaction. One-third of the space is left unassigned, and seesaws, hanging chairs, and hammocks are scattered around—seats you're unlikely to stay in for long. Constant movement encourages you to begin a different day each morning.

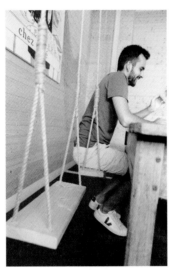

Roast a chicken

At My Little Paris, eating is an obsession. After all, any problem can be resolved around a good roast chicken, thanks to the free-flowing discussions it encourages. This is Marion's specialty: the My Little Paris chef regularly comes into the office to cook up a storm. There's a total of six kitchens, one on each floor. And sprinkled around the desks are those famous mugs adorned with drawings of individual employees.

“Did you try refreshing your cache?” ▶

*“It'll be OK once it's in production,” “The site
doesn't work,” “It's because of the varnish,”
“I won't do it because it's ugly,” etc. On the technical
team's floor, the kitchen walls are covered with self-
deprecatingly humorous quotes.*

Decorating with a story

The office is designed in such a way that it traces the story of My Little Paris. Visitors get a picture of how the start-up works by following a path through the company's various phases and activities. More effective than a PowerPoint presentation, it's storytelling as applied to interior design.

Slow office

Located high atop the offices, the terrace looks out over the rooftops toward the Sacré-Coeur. The top floor is an open space reserved for "slow work," creative dreaming, and in-depth projects that require long periods of concentration. It's the place where everything slows down: the pace, the teams, the conversation.

En train
de changer
le monde

↓

"
ccepte
grande
enture
tre moi
"

Meet me in the dreamery

To get some quiet time alone or hold a small meeting, there's always the dreamery: a former office that's been converted into a giant bed. A thick mattress perched on drawers full of pillows and blankets takes up the entire room.

Don't sit down

At first, teams used to gather around this long table, which was custom-made to fill the greenhouse. Communication was immediate and easy. Now that there are 130 people spread across ten locations, these days information is shared via short meetings like the "stand-up meeting," a five-minute morning briefing during which no one is allowed to sit down.

ROSA AND RICHARD

Caretaking

———

Rosa and Richard look after everything and everyone on a daily basis—from the plants that grow on the rooftop terrace to the interior design that changes every six months. Richard builds forts, converts chairs into seesaws, and transforms meeting rooms into dreameries, while Rosa ensures that the offices are welcoming and inspiring every single morning. She even puts fresh flowers on every floor once a week. She's like the keeper of the temple.

my
little

KANAKO

Head in the Stars

When she was little, Kanako dreamed of being an astronaut.
In the end, she touched down in France in 2005. She's been
the illustrator for My Little Paris since its very beginning.
Once a week, she installs her studio in the office, bringing
all her brushes and watercolors with her. Kanako produces
all her drawings on a single sheet of paper, almost like a
miniaturist. The only technology she allows herself when
she's drawing is a mini-scanner that fits into her purse and
enables her to send high-definition images anywhere at any
time—which is very practical when you're lingering on bistro
terraces sketching passersby.

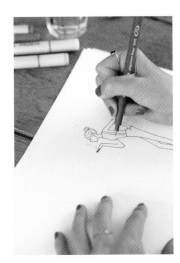

TOKYO

A Jumble of Frenchness in Omotesando

———

A terrace lined with deck chairs. A kitchen, a bedroom, and even a bathroom. Colors and drawings everywhere. The space teeters on the edge of chaos. The My Little Paris Toyko office is a surprise to first-time Japanese visitors: it's nothing like the usual working environment of the "salaryman."

And yet this is where My Little Paris based its successful expansion into Asia. Every month since 2014, the start-up has sent its My Little Box, full of surprises, accessories, and beauty products, to thousands of Japanese women who are in love with Paris. Today, a team of ten manages the group's Japanese branch, located in Omotesando, a very chic neighborhood more than a little shaken up by "Parisian habits."

Like the Berlin and Paris offices, the Tokyo location welcomes subscribers to monthly events where they are invited to share their opinions about the boxes they've received. Volunteers scramble to spend an evening in this Parisian-style apartment opened by My Little Box.

BERLIN

Backstage at the Opera

The magic of the opera lies in the hours and hours of behind-the-scenes work that vanish into thin air as soon as the curtain rises, to be replaced by emotional thrills. In the Berlin offices, located in the former opera workshops, the My Little Box Germany team also prepares its own little performance: the unveiling, once a month, of the box for subscribers.

The former workshops have been transformed into a perfectly Parisian apartment where, every month, one lucky subscriber is invited to spend the night. In the morning, he or she discovers My Little Box products waiting on the dressing table in the bedroom. There are also fresh croissants in the kitchen, needless to say.

MY LITTLE
Address Book

If you're stepping into the living rooms of Parisians in the know,
you may as well follow them to their favorite spots in the city.
Neighborhood restaurants recommended by word of mouth,
secret gardens for a taste of the countryside,
hidden corners worth crossing the capital for:
all the best addresses in town are here.

Lola

- **SANUKIYA RESTAURANT**: For the finest *kitsune udon* with fried tofu in Paris. *9, rue d'Argenteuil, Paris 1ᵉʳ*

- **LA STATION AT LA GARE DES MINES**: For those nights out where standards go out the window. You'll run into guys dressed as Teletubbies next to girls in swimsuits and sneakers; a place where you're free to do what you like without judgment. *29, avenue de la Porte d'Aubervilliers, Paris 18ᵉ*

- **EPISODE**: More under-the-radar than the vintage shops in the Marais. No one ever leaves empty-handed. *12–16, rue Tiquetonne, Paris 2ᵉ*

Clémentine

- **THE TROCADÉRO AQUARIUM**: Slip on a pair of headphones and be transported by the mammalian marine ballet taking place overhead. It's good for daydreaming and gaining some perspective. *Trocadéro, Paris 16ᵉ*

- **LIBRAIRIE JUNKU**: Practically all the books here are in Japanese, but I like things I don't understand. The books are pretty, and the atmosphere is calm and studious. It's a beautiful place in which to get lost and find yourself again. *18, rue des Pyramides, Paris 1ᵉʳ*

- **THE GALLERY OF EVOLUTION AT THE MUSEUM NATIONAL D'HISTOIRE NATURELLE**: It's fascinating and dreamlike; it reminds you we're just grains of sand. *57, rue Cuvier, Paris 5ᵉ*

Julia

- **VANTRE**: A gourmet bistro that's nicely low-key, despite its well-stocked wine list and its to-die-for gnocchi with sage butter. Beyoncé loves them. *19, rue de la Fontaine au Roi, Paris 11ᵉ*

- **LA CORDONNERIE DES ABBESSES**: The owner of this shoe-repair shop wears his heart on his sleeve and a smile on his face. He's always giving me gifts and discounts, though I don't really know him. That's my idea of a neighborhood. *48, rue des Abbesses, Paris 18ᵉ*

- **THE CHOUQUETTES AT ALEXINE**: After an in-depth investigation into every puff pastry in Paris, these take the cake. They're crunchy on top, with just the right amount of sugar—and, most importantly, they're super-soft on the inside. *40, rue Lepic, Paris 18ᵉ*

Inès

- **THE VIEW FROM RUE LAFFITE**: In a very loud neighborhood, on a busy boulevard, this is a haven of peace. From this vantage point, Notre-Dame-de-Lorette lines up with the Sacré-Coeur; it's pure magic. *Rue Laffite, Paris 9ᵉ*

- **THE PALAIS DE TOYKO**: You can still get lost here, even after ten visits. It challenges your idea of art and encourages reflection. You can talk to strangers, dance, climb a sculpture made of adhesive tape, and more. And I've even seen my grandmother perform there. *13, avenue du Président Wilson, Paris 16ᵉ*

- **TEN BELLES CAFÉ**: First thing in the morning, I grab a coffee from this place and drink it canal-side in the sun, with a newspaper. Next step: bring a deck chair. *10, rue de la Grange-aux-Belles, Paris 10ᵉ*

Maxime

- **GYPSY JAZZ HEAVYWEIGHTS AT LES PETITS JOUEURS**: Concerts take place in this former garage. You can show up alone, as a couple, or with a dozen friends—there's always room. And the food is excellent. *59, rue de Mouzaïa, Paris 19ᵉ*

- **THE AU VIEUX CAMPEUR STORE**: Because it's a landmark for any self-respecting trailblazing adventurer. You'll find everything here, from the latest Australian hiking backpack to freeze-dried muesli that's (almost) as good as the homemade kind. *2, rue Latran, Paris 5ᵉ*

- **L'ÉCUME DES PAGES**: Open until midnight, this bookstore is perfect for satisfying those nocturnal reading urges. *174, boulevard Saint-Germain, Paris 6ᵉ*

Lili

- **THE GARDEN AT THE MUSÉE DE LA VIE ROMANTIQUE**: A classic. Plus, the tearoom Rose Bakery just set up shop there. *16, rue Chaptal, Paris 9ᵉ*

- **YEN**: This is *the* Japanese restaurant for buckwheat soba. *22, rue Saint-Benoît, Paris 6ᵉ*

- **YOGA SATNAM STUDIO IN MONTMARTRE**: It's very small, it offers Kundalini yoga, and it was opened by Parisian yoga star Anne Bianchi. I never miss a session. *7, impasse Marie Blanche, Paris 18ᵉ*

Ana

- **ARÔM FLORIST**: Here, you pay by the flower. If you want a peony, and just one peony, they'll base a whole bouquet around the flower, and it's included in the price. *73, avenue Ledru-Rollin, Paris 12ᵉ*

- **THE DISPLAY AT LA TERRASSE DE GUTENBERG**: A neighborhood bookstore that's always well stocked with philosophy and art titles. The team has a taste for beautiful books, and their advice is spot-on. *9, rue Emilio Castelar, Paris 12ᵉ*

- **SATURDAY MORNING COFFEE AT CAFÉ CHARLETTE**: With a view of the organ-grinder and the stall overflowing with flowers. Afterwards, I shop for groceries at the Marché d'Aligre: fruit, vegetables, bread, chicken, antiques, flowers—the whole shebang. *11, rue d'Aligre, Paris 12ᵉ*

Enora

- **LES FLEURS**: At this shop, flea-market furniture cuddles up to cactuses, and demijohns flirt with armfuls of roses. This is where I get all my dried flowers. *5, rue Trousseau, Paris 11ᵉ*

- **NORWEGIAN EGGS AT CHEZ MARCEL**: Not only is this restaurant tucked away in the Villa Léandre, a little Parisian paradise a stone's throw from Montmartre, but the eggs here form the basis of any successful brunch. *23, rue des Dames, Paris 17ᵉ*

- **THE FOLIE-TITON GARDEN**: This is where I like to relax after succumbing to the chocolate-hazelnut marble cake at the Cyril Lignac patisserie, just across the street. *28, rue Chanzy, Paris 11ᵉ*

Diane

- **THE LEMON TART AT LADURÉE**: The rich crust garnished with a delicious lemon cream and topped with luscious meringue sprinkled with lime zest is a real pleasure! The different shades of yellow remind me of pure sunshine. *16–18, rue Royale, Paris 8ᵉ*

- **DELAVILLE CAFÉ**: This café is full of history. Imagine Paris society in the early 1900s. People strolled along the Grands Boulevards and stopped at Marguery, founded in 1860, a meeting place for artists, society women, and influential men. In 2015, the first two floors were entirely renovated and have become my headquarters. *34–36, boulevard de Bonne Nouvelle, Paris 10ᵉ*

- **THE STAIRCASE AT THE HOXTON HOTEL**: It looks as if it's suspended in mid-air. *30–32, rue du Sentier, Paris 2ᵉ*

Céline

- **LE SOURIRE DE SAIGON RESTAURANT**: Just three minutes from home, and I find myself in Vietnam. The rice is sticky, cooked and served in a bamboo stalk, and the waitstaff wear traditional outfits. It's perfect for a romantic dinner. *54, rue du Mont-Ceris, Paris 18ᵉ*

- **THE VIEWS FROM THE GARDENS AT THE MUSÉE DE MONTMARTRE**: Whether you're in the first garden, where you can admire one of Montmartre's water reservoirs and the glass roof of the Utrillo workshop, or in the garden below overlooking the vineyard, the panoramic view is incredible. *12, rue Cortot, Paris 18ᵉ*

- **THE GARDEN AT THE MUSÉE DU QUAI BRANLY**: Designed by Gilles Clément, where wild plants and biodiversity take center stage. *37, quai Branly, Paris 7ᵉ*

Jean-Nicolas

- **LE BON COIN RESTAURANT**: A typically French restaurant with a timeless hole-in-the-wall feel that's been run by the same family from Auvergne for five generations. The perfect start to any weekend. *49, rue des Cloys, Paris 18ᵉ*

- **TOAST AT THE COUNTER**: What's great about Paris is that you can down a few slices of toast at any neighborhood bar. It's a necessary ritual for those blurry mornings when you need to take stock while slathering toast with butter and jam.

- **THE JINJI STORE FOR MEN**: The best selection of American and Japanese denim that I know of, with a couch where visitors can set the world to rights with Julien and Renaldo, the founders. *22, rue des Canettes, Paris 6ᵉ*

Delphine

- **THE MARCHÉ D'ALIGRE**: For its ambience, its hoopla, its colors, and its smells. It's one of my required Sunday stops: I grab my basket and enjoy my grocery shopping as an activity in its own right. *Place d'Aligre, Paris 12ᵉ*

- **THE DISPLAY AT AILLEURS**: This design shop just downstairs from my place has a window display that has fascinated me since I moved here. *17, rue Saint-Nicolas, Paris 12ᵉ*

- **LA TRAVERSÉE RESTAURANT**: I love everything here—the staff, the menu, the products, the way the plates look. It's perfect. *2, rue Ramey, Paris 18ᵉ*

Pauline

- **GUERRISOL THRIFT SHOP**: I pay a visit to all seven Paris branches several times a week for my job, but also just out of fascination. Sometimes I give myself a rest by rummaging around in more classic thrift shops, like Chinemachine on rue des Martyrs. *96, boulevard Barbès, Paris 18ᵉ*

- **LA VIEILLE PIE CAFÉ**: An old-fashioned corner bar where I like to work, surrounded by the background sounds of real life that help me concentrate. *24, rue Pajol, Paris 18ᵉ*

- **LES ROUTIERS RESTAURANT**: Like the name suggests, this restaurant, located at the end of boulevard de la Chapelle, not far from the A1 highway, was for a long time one of the few places for truckers in the capital. It still brings together hearty eaters and regulars in a no-fuss atmosphere. They don't make 'em like this anymore! *50 bis, rue Marx Dormory, Paris 18ᵉ*

Marie

- **LA BOULANGERIE VERTE**: All the bakeries on rue des Martyrs fight for the title of best baguette, best chouquette, best this or that. La Boulangerie Verte has something that none of the others have: Floriane, the baker. She always has a kind word to lift the spirits. I head to her shop for bread and optimism. *60, rue des Martyrs, Paris 9ᵉ*

- **THE THÉÂTRE DU ROND POINT**: It's the best bet in Paris; it has never disappointed me. I can go see any show at random in the knowledge that it will be superb. *2 bis, avenue Franklin Delano Roosevelt, Paris 8ᵉ*

- **ISANA**: A friend runs this restaurant located down the street. It feels like home—but in Latin America! Jean-René, the owner, always makes us outrageous cocktails, and the empanadas are to die for. *7, rue Bourdaloue, Paris 9ᵉ*

Julia

- **LE COMPTOIR DU RELAIS SAINT-GERMAIN**: It feels like the best tapas-bistro in the world, with a unique atmosphere where two hundred people cram into 320 square feet (30 square meters) shouting their orders at waiters who manage to both hear and serve them. *9, carrefour de l'Odéon, Paris 6ᵉ*

- **TISSUS REINE AT THE SAINT-PIERRE MARKET**: I go bargain hunting for my best fabrics here, for both professional and personal projects. *3–5, place Saint-Pierre, Paris 18ᵉ*

- **LE FRUIT DÉFENDU RESTAURANT**: You have to get out of Paris to find this three-century-old establishment. It used to be an inn, then a chic dance hall, and today it's a restaurant: in the summer, eat along the waterside, under the lanterns; in the winter, huddle around the fireplace in the library. *80, boulevard de Belle Rive, Rueil-Malmaison*

Margot

- **LES PETITS MITRONS BAKERY**: The window display is overflowing with the kind of tarts that grandma makes, and their cookies are the best in Paris: crispy at the edges, barely cooked on the inside. I used to buy one every day for my afterschool snack when I was a kid. It's my Proustian madeleine. *26, rue Lepic, Paris 18ᵉ*

- **RUE LEPIC**: I grew up here. I lived at number 54, in a building where Van Gogh stayed for a few months. There were always hordes of tourists crowding around my doorstep. I wanted to do a little curtesy for them every time I went out. *Rue Lepic, Paris 18ᵉ*

- **THE SURPRISE PHOTOBOOTH**: Wedged between two buildings, it seems to have appeared out of nowhere, and it's the only booth in Paris to take truly beautiful, old-fashioned photos. *53, rue des Trois Frères, Paris 18ᵉ*

Fanny

- **DEYROLLE**: A cabinet of curiosities, stuffed animals (all died from natural causes, rest assured), and old school maps. On the ground floor, you'll also find the chicest garden tools in Paris, by the very charming Prince Jardinier. *46, rue du Bac, Paris 7ᵉ*

- **THE DELACROIX PAINTING AT SAINT-SULPICE CHURCH**: This painting is something of a personal pilgrimage for me. It depicts Jacob's struggle with the angel, and, if you look closely, it's more like a dance. I stop by to see it whenever I'm in the area. *Saint-Sulpice Church, Paris 6ᵉ*

- **LE FUMOIR**: Ask Eric, the barman, for a Singapore Sling. He'll also do magic tricks for you after 11 p.m. (if the place isn't too busy). Perfect for a romantic dinner in the library. *6, rue de l'Amiral de Coligny, Paris 1ᵉʳ*

Usha

- **THE VIEW FROM THE CENTRE GEORGES POMPIDOU**: A 360-degree panoramic view of Paris, its monuments, rooftops, the river, and the faraway murmur of Parisians going about their lives. Classic but also unique. *Place Georges-Pompidou, Paris 4ᵉ*

- **RUE DU FAUBOURG SAINT-DENIS**: An incredible illustration of the diversity of Paris. You'll find everything here: the excellent restaurant 52, the best burger in Paris at Paris-New York, the pizzeria Sette, and very good fresh vegetables. *Paris 10ᵉ*

- **LE RICHER**: I never get tired of this restaurant. It's the best value for money in Paris and, since it expanded last year, you can go there on a whim. They don't take reservations; that way, everyone has a chance to grab a table. *2, rue Richer, Paris 9ᵉ*

Charles

- **THE EIGHTEENTH**: My home, my friends, and my habits are based in this arrondissement, which resembles a mythical idea of Paris I had when I was growing up as a teenager in the country. This neighborhood is here to stay.

- **THE BAR AT LE RÊVE**: An institution on the Butte, frequented by regulars. You have to experience it at least once. The interiors have remained unchanged for several decades, and a semblance of social diversity persists. You can just pop in and grab a glass standing up. *89, rue Caulaincourt, Paris 18ᵉ*

- **LES PUCES**: This is where I turned my passion into a profession when I opened my four Tombées du Camion locations in the Marché Vernaison. They're a little exotic, populated with antiquated objects. *Marché de Vernaison, 99, rue des Rosiers, Row 1, Stalls 29, 30, 31, and Row 3, Stalls 107 and 108 bis, 93400 Saint-Ouen*

Clémence

- **CHEZ SIMONE**: Hidden in a Haussmann-style apartment with a view, this is a place where you can eat, sweat, and meet other sporty types. You can also take classes with Clélia Edouard, who motivates everyone to challenge themselves and test their limits. *226, rue de Saint-Denis, Paris 2ᵉ*

- **CHAMBELLAND BAKERY**: There's no shortage of bakeries in Paris. But at this one the baker grinds his own rice flour to make his gluten-free bread. You'll also find the Marquise de Popincourt and her lemon tart done just right. *14, rue Ternaux, Paris 11ᵉ*

- **THE VIEW OF THE SEINE RIVER FROM THE PONT NEUF**: I love running along the quays, and I always stop here, even if my stopwatch is still going. It's breathtaking at any hour. *Paris 1ᵉ*

Marion

- **THE MUSÉE NISSIM DE CAMONDO**: One of the most touching museums in Paris. It's a collection of eighteenth-century art objects and the jewel of the Parc Monceau neighborhood. But it's also the story of a rich family between the late nineteenth century and World War II, with its tragedies, its secrets, and even its kitchen, straight out of Downton Abbey. *63, rue de Monceau, Paris 8ᵉ*

- **E. DEHILLERIN**: Stepping into this kitchen supply store is like finding yourself in a Balzac novel. Copper pots, old-fashioned pans, real pastry whisks—they have everything, including guys in grey smocks to help you. It's deliciously nineteenth century. *18–20, rue Coquillière, Paris 1ᵉʳ*

- **THE JACQUES GENIN PATISSERIE**: Come here for the best custard tart ever, with its unbeatable rich cream filling, as thick as a cheesecake. *133, rue de Turenne, Paris 3ᵉ*

Émile

- **LADJI'S STALL AT LES PUCES**: Ladji dances and sings all day long, surrounded by his vintage items and African vinyl records. Many of my musical discoveries I owe to him.
Les Puces de Paris Saint-Ouen, Saint-Ouen

- **RUE DE CLIGNANCOURT**: This is the hip-hop musician Doc Gynéco's street; more importantly, it turns into rue Ramey, which leads to a village hidden on the other side of the Butte. Try it and see.
Paris 18ᵉ

- **BODRUM'S KEBABS**: The best in Paris, made with the owner's homemade bread and meat marinated for hours by his wife. But you've been warned: be prepared for a long line at all hours.
43, rue des Batignolles, Paris 17ᵉ

Marie

- **MAMICHE**: At this bakery, the classics are given a decadent twist. There are baguettes, but they have added chocolate and salted-butter chips. There are brioches, too, but they're marbled with chocolate. It's to die for. *45, rue Condorcet, Paris 9ᵉ*

- **LE JEU DE PAUME**: Go for its photography exhibitions, which are always a pleasant surprise. And follow up with a stroll in the Tuileries gardens. *1, place de la Concorde, Paris 8ᵉ*

- **L'ÉTABLISIENNE**: This workshop, perfumed with sawdust, is run by two enthusiastic woodworkers. When we're not making our own furniture in our living room, we like dropping by.
88, boulevard de Picpus, Paris 12ᵉ

Sibylle

- **A NIGHT ON THE INVALIDES ESPLANADE**: The view is incredible, and yet it's often deserted, which is rare in Paris. There's a little bench at the metro exit, at the intersection with rue Saint-Dominique, where I like to sit when I need some peace.
Place des Invalides, Paris 7ᵉ

- **A CROISSANT FROM CHEZ JULHÈS**: Aside from being delicious, it's warm and comes wrapped in paper stamped "Julhès." Whenever I get one, I feel as though I'm buying myself a present.
60, rue du Faubourg Saint-Denis, Paris 10ᵉ

- **THE FLOATING TERRACE AT PANAME BREWING COMPANY**: It's easy to forget you're in Paris here. The beer is cold, the staff pleasant, and the design hipster (though the atmosphere isn't). I used to live just next door, so it was my headquarters.
41 bis, quai de la Loire, Paris 19ᵉ

Fany

- **THE SMALLEST AND BEST COBBLER IN PARIS**: His shop is squeezed into just 26 square feet (8 square meters), and he's located in the doorway at number *12, rue Duphot, Paris 1er*

- **THE SECRET POOL AT THE MINISTRY OF THE ARMED FORCES**: The pool is open to the public but is considered a protected military area. You have to request a pass from the government, and you'll be investigated before you're allowed to swim in the pool. *11, avenue de la Porte de Sèvres, Paris 15e*

- **LADDA**: My favorite massage studio, hidden under the rooftops. *32, rue du Paradis, Paris 10e*

Maeva

- **THE BANKS OF THE CANAL DE L'OURCQ**: I go here for my Sunday morning jog. The canal is nearly overflowing, and no one's out yet. People are late risers in this part of town. *Paris 19e*

- **A DRINK AT MAISON-MAISON**: The burrata–rosé combo is the key to a successful night. It makes any evening feel like a vacation, even during the week. *Facing 16, quai du Louvre, Paris 1er*

Anne Flore

- **THE GARDEN AT THE MUSÉE DE MONTMARTRE**: If you have an annual membership, you can visit all year round, enjoying a haven of green all to yourself. Every Sunday morning when the weather is nice, I have a coffee here and read the paper. *12, rue Cortot, Paris 18e*

- **CINABRE**: A store that reflects the transformation under way in the tenth arrondissement, which is becoming increasingly popular—and not only for its restaurants. You'll find accessories for men made in France: bowties, ties, bags, etc. Okay, it's my husband's store, but it was also included in the *Louis Vuitton Guide*. Go see the gorilla and the robots: you'll soon get the picture. *20, rue d'Hauteville, Paris 10e*

- **THE TOP FLOOR OF BRASSERIE BARBÈS**: In Paris, we're always looking for a bar with good music where we can dance. This place, with its bay window, Mehdi on the turntables, and Steve at the bar, might well be it. *2, boulevard Barbès, Paris 18e*

Perla

- **THE PONT ALEXANDRE III**: Cross this bridge in the early morning to admire the beauty of Paris, the only capital I love living in. Which is just as well—I've been here fifty-two years. *Paris 8ᵉ*

- **BEAUBOURG**: I love visiting at any hour, whatever exhibition is on, with my partner or a friend. I rarely leave without an idea, without feeling inspired. *Place Georges-Pompidou, Paris 4ᵉ*

- **LE BALZAC**: The best thing about this movie theater, a ten-minute walk from my house, is going there alone. Early in the morning. Why does such a thing only exist in Paris? No idea. *1, rue Balzac, Paris 8ᵉ*

Marie-Yaé

- **GO FROM BIR HAKEIM TO PASSY ON LINE 6**: This station is surreal!

- **BENTOS AT JUJI-YA**: You can eat them either in the Tuileries or in the garden across from the Institut National d'Histoire de l'Art (National Institute of Art History). *46, rue Sainte-Anne, Paris 2ᵉ*

- **THE FRANÇOISE SAGAN LIBRARY**: Its palm trees offer a taste of Italy in Paris on a horrible street off boulevard Magenta. It has an incredible story, too: it was a leper house, a women's prison during the Revolution, and then a hospital for prostitutes in the nineteenth century. *8, rue Léon Schwartzenberg, Paris 10ᵉ*

Céline

- **DU PAIN ET DES IDÉES BAKERY**: I was born and raised in a bakery. I'm capable of crossing Paris just for a bit of bread, in this case Christophe Vasseur's *pain des amis*, which has an almost smoky flavor. With tomatoes and burrata, it's heaven. *34, rue Yves Toudic, Paris 10ᵉ*

- **YOGA WITH CAROLINE BÉNÉZET**: I've been practicing Kundalini yoga for six years, which I discovered thanks to this incredible teacher. Three weeks after we'd met, I followed her to an ashram in India. I'd recommend her classes, which are held throughout Paris.

- **CAPITAINE RESTAURANT**: I've been mostly vegetarian for five years, but I have three scouts who tell me when something's worth breaking the rules for. It might happen twice a year. The last time it was at Capitaine, where killer tapas are served as shared starters. It was the pork meatballs with mayonnaise that made me crack. *4, impasse Guéménée, Paris 4ᵉ*

Kanako

- **THE ROOFTOP TEACHING HIVE**: The teaching hive at Villa Bosquet hosts beekeeping workshops on Diane's rooftop terrace (p. 293). Climbing up to this garden high above Paris to gather honey is almost too French for this Japanese girl!
Chez Jos, 28, boulevard Bonne Nouvelle, Paris 10ᵉ

- **HARRY'S BAR**: A century-old Paris institution that never changes, with waiters in white jackets and the best cocktails in the capital, if you ask me. I stay all evening, nibbling on a hotdog between drinks.
5, rue Daunou, Paris 2ᵉ

- **TAEKO AT THE MARCHÉ DES ENFANTS ROUGES**: I like to pull up a chair at this Japanese restaurant after looking around the market and pillaging the truffle *saucisson* at Mangiamo Italiano.
39, rue de Bretagne, Paris 3ᵉ

Céline

- **RUE DU NIL**: A visit to all the Terroirs d'Avenir shops is obligatory. They're the kings of quality sourcing, and their produce makes up nearly 100 percent of my meals. Line-caught fish from Finistère, veal from the Basque Country, vegetables and herbs from the Val d'Oise—the products here are exceptional. *Paris 2ᵉ*

- **THE PONTOISE POOL**: I've made this my meditation space, where all my fears subside. The superb dressing rooms with their peepholes over the pool are a treat. This pool is a registered historical landmark. *19, rue de Pontoise, Paris 5ᵉ*

- **YARD WINE BAR**: I love this place because of the values of the owner, Clovis Ochin. Kindness, generosity, sharing, wonderful conversation, and more. Here, you eat well, drink well, and feel well.
6, rue de Mont-Louis, Paris 11ᵉ

Amandine

- **LES BUTTES CHAUMONT**: It's a little bit like the Central Park of Paris. You see everything here: guys reading poems on demand, groups doing tai chi, wedding brunches, and so on. I can wander around here for hours. *1, rue Botzaris, Paris 19ᵉ*

- **EVENINGS AT ROSA BONHEUR**: The owner likes people, and it shows. Her cheerful disposition affects the whole place, which is both poetic and festive. *2, avenue de la Cascade, Paris 19ᵉ*

- **THE HEART OF PARIS**: It always beats at a hundred miles a minute. I love knowing that something exceptional is going on somewhere in Paris: a magnificent play, an inspiring exhibition, a memorable celebration on the banks of the Seine, a moment of celebration in a neighborhood bar, and so on. It's magical. So why choose just one spot?

Editorial Direction: My Little Paris with
Guillaume Robert and
Kate Mascaro at Flammarion
Apartment Photography: Tomoko Yasuda
Office Photography: Lucie Sassiat
Illustrations: Kanako Kuno
Editor, English Edition: Sam Wythe
Translated from the French by
Kate Robinson
Copyediting: Penelope Isaac
Typesetting: Gravemaker+Scott
Proofreading: Sarah Kane
Production: Louisa Hanifi,
Christelle Lemonnier, and
Titouan Roland
Color Separation: IGS, L'Isle d'Espagnac
Printed in Slovenia by GPS Group

Originally published in French as *Chez les Parisiens:*
Appartements et bureaux créatifs à Paris
© Flammarion, S.A., Paris, 2018

English-language edition
© Flammarion, S.A., Paris, 2019

editions.flammarion.com

19 20 21 3 2 1

ISBN: 978-2-08-020400-4

Legal Deposit: 06/2019

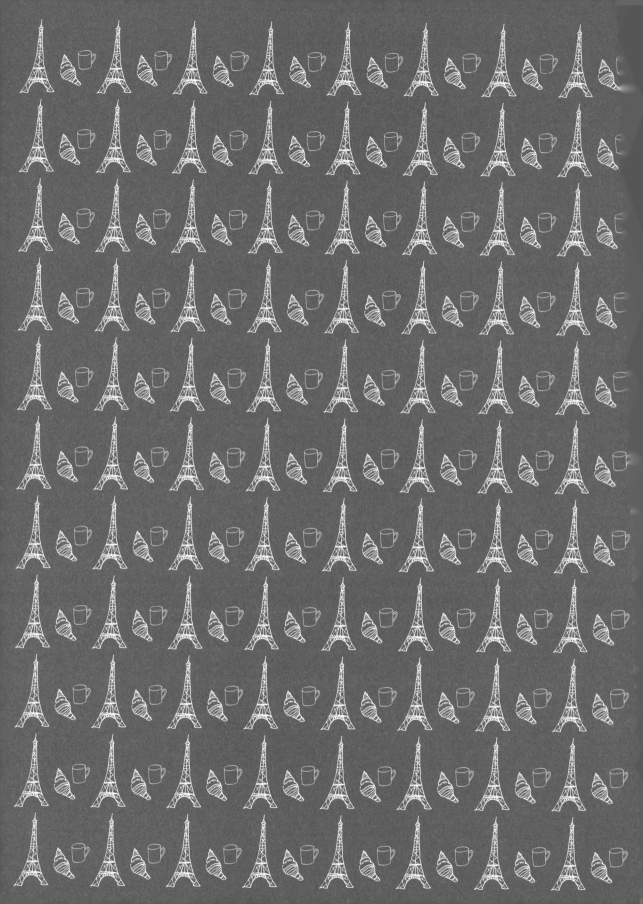